BUILDING CRAFTSMANSHIP
IN BRICK AND TILE
AND IN STONE SLATES

BUILDING CRAFTSMANSHIP
IN BRICK AND TILE
AND IN STONE SLATES

by

NATHANIEL LLOYD, O.B.E., F.S.A.

AUTHOR OF
A HISTORY OF ENGLISH BRICKWORK
AND OF
PRACTICAL BRICKWORK IN
*THE ENCYCLOPÆDIA
BRITANNICA, &c.*

CAMBRIDGE
AT THE UNIVERSITY PRESS
1929

CAMBRIDGE
UNIVERSITY PRESS

University Printing House, Cambridge CB2 8BS, United Kingdom

Published in the United States of America by Cambridge University Press, New York

Cambridge University Press is part of the University of Cambridge.

It furthers the University's mission by disseminating knowledge in the pursuit of education, learning and research at the highest international levels of excellence.

www.cambridge.org
Information on this title: www.cambridge.org/9781107673366

First published 1929
First paperback edition 2014

A catalogue record for this publication is available from the British Library

ISBN 978-1-107-67336-6 Paperback

PREFACE

I HOPE this little book may prove helpful to that daily increasing section of the public, lay and professional, which appreciates good craftsmanship.

I wish to express my profound gratitude to Sir Edwin Landseer Lutyens, R.A., who first inspired me to observe, practise and make known old and new ways of "right building"; also my sincere thanks to another friend, Mr H. Greville Montgomery, Hon. A.R.I.B.A., editor of *The Brick Builder*, etc., and to the Architectural Press, Ltd., whose loans of blocks have made possible the publication of this volume at a moderate price.

NATHANIEL LLOYD

GREAT DIXTER
NORTHIAM, SUSSEX
March 1929

CONTENTS

CRAFTSMANSHIP

There are buildings which charm us: others leave us cold. Often we cannot detect the elements which produce results that fill us with a sense of delight and satisfaction or those which have the contrary effect or, at least, which fail to inspire pleasure. How often do old buildings appeal to us and how seldom new ones! Amongst architects whose works possess the charm of old work is Sir Edwin L. Lutyens, one of the few living men to have penetrated the veil and discovered for himself those qualities which make old buildings what they are and who has succeeded in applying the same principles to his own works. Such subtle qualities are particularly noticeable in domestic buildings, in which we are quick to see their influence upon the whole, although unable to see "how it is done". Even those who are able to refer to building textbooks get no assistance, for none of them enter into such refinements, nor, indeed, trouble to expound them. Yet the thirst for such knowledge is apparent in the young Architect who has passed through the schools with distinction, in the Estate Agent who has to design cottages and estate buildings, in the Builder who aspires to something beyond the common practice, and especially in the Layman who contemplates having a house built for his own occupation and would appreciate those little touches, not necessarily entailing increased expenditure, which in some mysterious way confer charm and distinction upon a home.

For each and all of these, this book has been written. It tells what the eighteenth century book-writers would have called the "secrets" of good building, few of which are to be found in other books. They include illustrations from works of Sir Edwin Lutyens and other architects as well as examples from works of the old builders, now forgotten. Many illustrations are by photographs taken "close up", showing each stage of the work as well as the completed job. Where it was thought that greater clearness could be secured by measured drawings, these have been added.

Briefly, this may claim to be the first technical work to take cognisance of those elements which produce charm of effect in building construction.

I. TILED ROOFS

F EW, if any of us, can have failed to be captivated by the charm of old house roofs hung with plain tiles, the hips covered with "Granny" bonnets, set in mortar and crowned with semi-circular ridges. Time has done much for these roofs. He has softened their outlines, undulated their slopes and clothed them with lichens in his livery of green and purple and gold. There are, however, other factors, such as the materials of which the roofs are composed, and the manner in which they are constructed, which gave Time a good basis upon which to work. It may be of interest to consider exactly to what these old roofs owe their charm and how far it is possible to secure at least part of it for modern buildings.

PITCH

Many old roofs had a pitch of 60 deg., seldom less than 55 deg. That of the modern roof is generally 45 deg., which is the flattest pitch the textbooks allow for plain tiles. Unfortunately, a pitch of 45 deg. is the most unpleasing of all pitches. It is that which Sir Edwin Lutyens once described as "the ugly angle". A pitch of 30 deg. or less, for slates, if furnished with deep eaves, is satisfactory; 50 deg. for tiles is on the border line, but 45 deg. is anathema and must be avoided. A safe and pleasing pitch is 55 deg. Actually, 54 deg. 45 min. will be found practicable. This is an angle to which I shall refer again later, and is one for which it is convenient to have a set square made. It will be found that the other angle of this square, viz. 35 deg. 15 min., gives a good angle for the flatter pitch formed by the sprocket pieces (fig. 11) so the use of this square will facilitate quick, accurate and satisfactory detailing.

There is one detail which I have observed requires a pitch of 60 deg., and that is the little triangular gable, like that in fig. 3, where the pitch is 54 deg. 45 min., and is too squat entirely to please the eye. If the roof

pitch were flatter still, the effect would be more unpleasing, just as the steeper pitch of 60 deg. is more charming. Gablets in old cottage roofs are generally found in roofs of this pitch.

In old farmhouses one frequently sees the main roof carried down at some point from second-floor to first-floor level, to cover an extension of the ground floor for scullery or other offices. Probably with a view to obtaining greater floor area for the ground floor extension and possibly, also, with an eye to effect, the roof pitch of such extensions was always a little flatter (5 deg. perhaps) than that of the main roof. This change of pitch produced a very pleasing angle in the roof slope, the value of which may be seen by comparing figs. 5 and 6. Such change of pitch would be less necessary, however, from the visual standpoint, had the eaves at the bottom of the roof extension been swept to a bellcast by the use of sprocket pieces, as in figs. 3 and 4.

EAVES

This device (figs. 1, 2 and 11) of producing that upward sweep at the eaves termed bellcast by means of an eaves lath or tilting fillet for a slight tilt and by nailing sprocket pieces on the rafters for a greater sweep, though not always employed, is an ancient one. By the use of sprocket pieces to produce deep eaves, the projection is obtained with economy of rafter length at the expense of short pieces of quartering. An excellent and economical bellcast is produced by the use of pieces of 4 in. × 2 in., cut diagonally out of 8 in. lengths. Sprocket pieces also facilitate the setting of the wall plate well within the centre line of the wall and the resulting change to flatter pitch towards the eaves has the effect of making the lower edges of tiles *bite* closely against the tiles under them, so securing closer union just where it is most wanted. Such bite of the lower edges is further accentuated

FIG. 1. Middlefield, Great Shelford, Cambs., by Sir E. L. Lutyens, R.A.

FIG. 2. Kitchingham Farm, Robertsbridge, Sussex. Old-fashioned roof treatment.

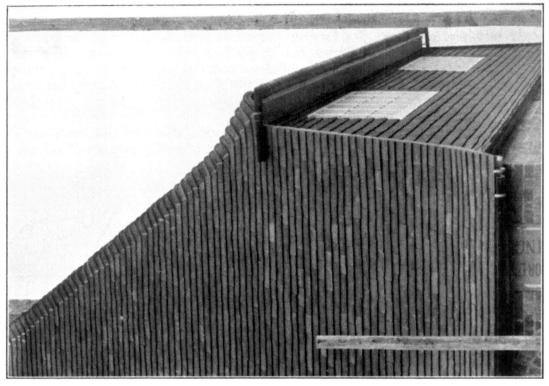

Fig. 4. Hip, verge and eaves.

Fig. 3. Gablet, hip and verge treatments.

by the eaves lath or tilting fillet and by the under-tile of the eaves course being bedded upside-down and also by these tiles having a pronounced set or curve, as shown in figs. 9, 11. The importance of the pleasing curve produced by such eaves-treatment can hardly be over-emphasised.

These unsymmetrical houses seldom had the eaves of all elevations at the same level (where there were angle posts, the wall

In this drawing, also, a tile soffit is shown. This consists of two tile courses, and it should be noted that the upper of these has greater projection than the lower. If there were three courses, each should have greater projection than that immediately below it.

UNDULATIONS

The undulations of old roofs are due to settlement of walls, sagging of rafters, decay

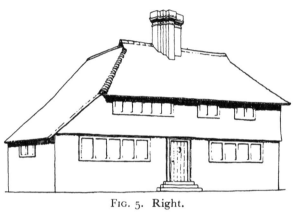

FIG. 5. Right.

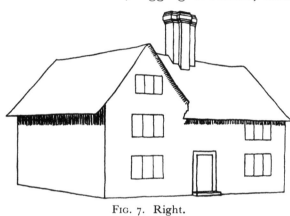

FIG. 7. Right.

FIG. 6. Wrong.

FIG. 8. Wrong.

plates met at different levels), nor were gables carried down exactly to meet the eaves. The treatment of fig. 7 is certainly more pleasing than that of the more conventional one in fig. 8, yet the former is seldom adopted in modern work.

In fig. 9 the facing of the 11 in. wall is finished with a three-course tile creasing. This rises the height of one brick course, but a single or double tile-creasing course is often conveniently introduced where something less than a whole brick course is required.

of rafter feet, sagging of tile laths or similar causes. Where a partition wall happens to have been carried up to the roof, the latter is supported at that point, though it may sink on each side and a hump is formed in the ridge and continued down the slope, as may be seen in the middle of the big roof of fig. 2. There is a limit to be observed in copying such effects, but the judicious use of 2 by 2 in. counter battens, nailed on the rafters at irregular intervals, before nailing the tile battens will prevent excessive uniformity.

Where the line of an old roof is continued over a new addition it is particularly necessary to adopt such treatment, without which an extremely hard and ugly looking change of roof slope may result.

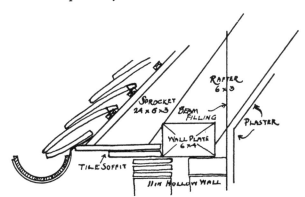

FIG. 9. Detail of eaves of a main roof.

Old tiles varied more than do even hand-made modern tiles, and the holes, with their wooden pins, were more irregular than nibs or nails. They were hung on riven oak laths, which were not precisely straight as are sawn battens. The combination of these factors produced variety which is much more pleasing than the mechanical accuracy of modern tiling. This, to some extent, may be overcome in marking off the gauge rod, which is a batten as long as the distance from ridge to eaves. Across it the tiler draws pencil lines the exact gauge his tiles are to be hung. If this is 3½ in. gauge, the lines will be that distance apart, and this batten, laid on the roof, guides the nailing of the tile battens or laths. To direct the tilers to vary the gauge is inadvisable, but if the gauge rod be marked for them, they will follow it slavishly. Variety may be introduced into the marking of the gauge rod so that the gauge is often a little more or a little less than 3½ in., thus, starting at the eaves: 3½, 3½, 3¼, 3¾, 3¾, 3¼, 3½, etc. The same number of courses will result, without mechanical regularity and the efficiency of the roof covering will not be materially affected. The roof in figs. 3, 4, 12, was treated in this way.

Old tiles were never made flat, but were curved in their length and often in their width. This curving is sometimes called the

"set" or "camber" of a tile, or a tile is said to have "housing" in its length or to be "hatched" in its breadth. The curve in length is valuable, as has already been pointed out, in causing the lower edge of a tile to bite down closely upon that under it, and so prevent driving rain or snow from blowing up underneath the tiles. The curve in width has a contrary effect: it is less common, but it does produce a happy effect of variety in the roof surface.

COLOUR AND TEXTURE

Perhaps the most important visual qualities in tiles are good colour and rough texture. No colours can compare with rich glowing reds. There is a large range of good reds, avoiding pale orange on the one hand, and bluish-purples on the other. What are

FIG. 10. Houses at Biddenden, Kent. Tile roof swept over oriel window.

called "antique" tiles (generally dull browns devised immediately to produce roofs of subdued colourings), are at their best when newly hung. As time passes, they become more and more sombre, and never assume the delightful colourings of the old roofs. If, however, red tiles (varying in tone according to the extent each has been fired) are used, the first rawness wears off in less than a couple of years; in five years they have acquired a beautiful variety of tones and colours, and each year thereafter (if their

tained tiny pebbles. In firing the tiles, the sand, which had become impressed into the surface of the clay, fell out, leaving just that roughness of surface which we call good texture and upon which lichens and mosses quickly grow. Such texture is incomparably superior to rough surfaces, such as are produced on bricks by scratching with wires and by other artificial devices.

The detail of eaves (fig. 11) shows 1 by $1\frac{1}{2}$ in. counter battens on felt over rough boarding. An alternative is to substitute

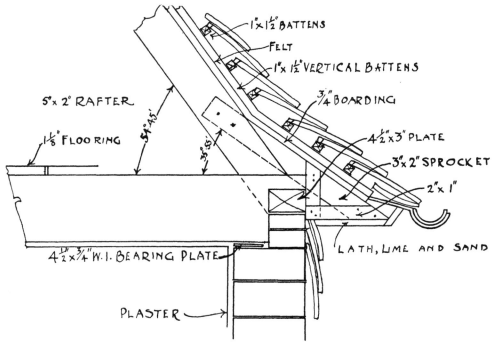

FIG. 11. The critical points of bellcast to roof and eaves treatment and finish of wall-tiling.
To soften the angle at change of pitch, the fourth course bridges the angle.

texture is good) they assume more variety of colour in browns, purples, golds, greens and greys of lichens and mosses—according to the aspect—through which the original reds of the burnt clay glow in the most delightful way.

To achieve such results, it is essential the tiles should have the right kind of surface upon which Time may do his beneficent work. This is so easy to obtain that it is surprising it should so often be lacking. The texture of the old tiles was got by the use of coarse sand for coating the clot of clay and sprinkling the mould. Often the sand con-

ordinary laths (which are cheaper) for these vertical battens as it is only necessary the tile (horizontal) battens should clear the felt that moisture may run down and out at the eaves.

Fig. 10 shows a practical and picturesque way of sweeping roof tiles over an oriel window.

VERGES

Modern practice is to use tile-and-a-half tiles in alternate courses at verges, etc., and certainly these produce a stronger result than the old method of employing half-tile "straights". When these tile-and-a-half tiles

FIG. 13. Wrong—and weak verge without undercloak.

FIG. 12. (a) Right—and strong verge with undercloak tiles. (b) The board over the head of the window frame temporarily supports the heading course of wall tiles bedded in cement.

FIG. 14.

FIG. 15.

FIG. 16.

match the other tiles, as in fig. 4, they are tolerable, but when they do not match, they are disfiguring.

From no roof, however finely cut the job may be, should be omitted the use of a tile undercloak, as shown in fig. 12. The economy effected by its omission is trifling, the necessity for earlier repair is certain. The verge is a weak spot both structurally and as being penetrable by weather. Rendering the verge with mortar or cement, as in fig. 13, is unsightly and is not an efficient substitute for the undercloak. Besides strengthening it, the undercloak, by slightly raising the verge, throws away from it the water flowing down the roof, and so prevents it being driven by wind between the verge and the wall. Incidentally, it produces a graceful, though slight, upward sweep at the verge which the photographs do not clearly show.

Where the use of sprocket pieces or of an eaves lath produces an upward curve at the eaves, tiles having the same curve, when laid

FIG. 17.

FIGS. 14–17. Various shapes of hip and ridge tiles.

FIG. 18. "Granny" bonnet hip tiles well set up and swept to a good bellcast.

concave side up, should be used for the under-cloak course, as may just be seen near the foot of the illustration in fig. 3.

Verge tiles should be bedded in hair mortar or cement as they are laid, and care taken that the mortar does not soil the tile edges, which should be left clean and red. To secure complete union between mortar and tiles, the tiles at eaves, hips, verges and ridges should be saturated with water when

HIP TILES

The current practice of making hip tiles exactly to the pitch of the roof, robs it of much of the charm imparted by the old-fashioned "Granny" bonnet hip tiles. Figs. 14 and 16 show front and side views of each type. Fig. 15 is a hip tile, of curve between the two. Figs. 3, 4, 12 show "Granny" bonnets on a roof, which has deep sprocketed eaves over

FIG. 19. Double hip, showing filling of ridge tile and of lowest hip tiles.

bedded, but it is always difficult to get work-men to do this. The verge of a large gable may project fully 3 in. beyond the wall face, i.e. about half the width of a tile. Of course, small gables, as of dormers, will require less projection and, in practice, it will be found that, where walls are hung with weather tiling, the thickness of this reduces the effec-tive projection of the roof verge to less than 2 in.

the first floor windows in front, but where the side roof is continued down over the ground floor. As the sprocket pieces can only be nailed to the front rafters, the hip tiles must sweep round from the hip rafter to the front, as shown in figs. 3, 12. This particular case often proves puzzling both to carpenters and tilers, who, if allowed to do so, would bring the hip tiles down the hip rafter to its foot and cobble the return of the eaves as best they could. The unsightly appearance of a double depth of mortar under the lowest hip tile may be avoided by the insertion of a small curved piece of hip tile, dividing it into two, as shown in figs. 3, 4, 12, 19. Another finish is by the use of a tile tongue 2 in. wide, which protrudes over the angle, and this is particularly suitable when the junction of the under-eaves-course tiles forms a sharp angle, as in fig. 18, instead of being rounded as in fig. 19.

FIG. 20. Swept valley-tiles cut to wedge shapes.

RIDGE TILES

The half-round ridge tile and its variants, as shown in fig. 17, are unsurpassed, and serrated or crested ridges may be left to such speculative builders as may still think them beautiful. For some positions the segmental ridge tile, as in fig. 19, is better suited than the full half-round, especially where it is desired this should bed down closely. There are several devices for filling in the open

end of the ridge tile at hipped gables. If mortar only is used, the face of this should be kept back ½ in. from the end of the ridge tile, so leaving a projecting margin of tile, as in fig. 51, which casts a pleasing shadow. Another method is to fill in the space with the butt of a wine or beer bottle, or a piece of plain tile may be cut to a semicircle, so as (with a ½ in. joint all round) exactly to fill the opening, but best of all, perhaps, is to fill with plain tiles, laid flat with ½ in. joints, as in fig. 19. These may be flush with the end of the ridge tile as in fig. 19 or set back half-an-inch as in fig. 25.

It is important that ridge tiles should be slightly tilted upwards at the extremities of

FIG. 21. Two faults are here illustrated. (1) The ridge tiles are not bedded down sufficiently closely. (2) The heading course of plain tiles and the hip tile of that course dip downwards instead of being tilted up slightly (as are those in the two courses below) to help the tilting of the end ridge tile.

a ridge, whether these occur at the junction with chimneys, as in figs. 3, 10, or at the apices of gables. The improved appearance as compared with a perfectly straight line is obvious; water is thrown off from vulnerable points, and as the last ridge is usually wedged in tightly against the brickwork, greater strength is secured.

Ridge tiles should be well and carefully bedded in hair mortar or cement, which should not be visible, even from below. A slight upward tilt of the end ridge tiles is sound construction as well as pleasing in appearance, but this must be obtained without showing the mortar on which the ridge is bedded. The dip of the hip tile of the heading course in fig. 21 should have been a slight rise. The more closely ridge tiles "sit down" on the heading courses of plain tiles the more secure they are likely to be. In a very exposed situation or where the lead of a flat roof finishes under one side of the ridge, lead tacks or clips may be brought through between the ridge tiles and turned 1½ in. over them. These tacks may be provided between every ridge tile or at such intervals as may seem necessary.

VALLEYS

The purpose-made valley tile is convenient and inexpensive, but it cannot compare for appearance with a swept valley, where an easy curve has been formed by the use of a wide valley board and the plain tiles cut to the necessary shapes. Such valleys do not require lead, but the tile cutting is slow work and very trying to the tilers' hands. Fig. 20 shows tile swept valleys in a main roof and at the junction of dormers with the main roof.

Another valley treatment, not so widely known, is what has been named the "Laced Valley", as shown in fig. 22, together with a drawing showing the construction, fig. 23. The foundation is an 11 in. valley board on the hip rafter. Upon this board tile-and-a-half tiles are laid diagonally. Up to the two lower edges of these the courses of plain tiles sweep. The photograph is of a roof in a housing scheme at Eltham. Similar valleys were adopted in the housing scheme at Stanmore, Hants. The operation is inexpensive and easily learned by workmen, who in time become so skilful as to lace main-roof valleys without cutting or shaping a single tile.

Pantiles form a good wall coping, which effectually protects peach and other fruit trees trained against the wall below. Fig. 24 shows one method of stopping an end which, however, is not so good a finish as the more elaborate hipped treatment illustrated in fig. 25. These two figures show also the effects at external angles, while fig. 26 is a large detail of an internal angle, the treatment of which will vary as the points at

which the pantiles happen to intersect. The drawing, fig. 27, is a section of this coping. It will be found convenient first to cast the breeze concrete to the desired triangular section, in 2 or 3 ft. lengths, and then to bed these on the wall ready to receive the pantiles.

When pantiles are very hard (and generally they seem to be much harder and tougher than plain tiles) they are difficult to cut to

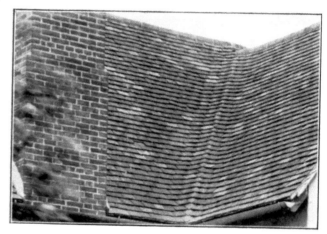

FIG. 22. Laced valley in a housing scheme.

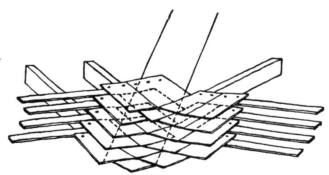

FIG. 23. Method of working laced valley.

a mitre: hence the relatively wide joints seen in figs. 25 and 26. There is, however, something very attractive in the curves of these external angles, as may be seen in figs. 24 and 25. Indeed, without any intention to do so, they recall features with which one is familiar in illustrations of Chinese roofs. They also suggest that other uses may be found for pantiles, which would prove equally pleasing, provided they were used structurally and not as mere ornaments. One legitimate

FIG. 24. Pantile wall coping: open end filled with plain tiles.

FIG. 25. Pantile wall coping: end hipped and pantiles mitred at hips.

FIG. 26. Pantile wall coping: internal angle.

use is to employ pantiles for a fascia, as in fig. 28, tailing in with cement breeze to which they also adhere. Of course, the pantiles require support until the breeze has set.

Figs. 24, 25, 26 and 27 also show the old and proper way of filling up the hollow of a pantile by a short ½ plain tile lying on a 10 in. ¼ plain tile. Not only do these fill up a space usually made unsightly by much mortar but they also provide a firm and continuous base upon which to bed the ridge tiles. This bedding is better done in fig. 24 than in figs. 25 and 26, where too much mortar is seen.

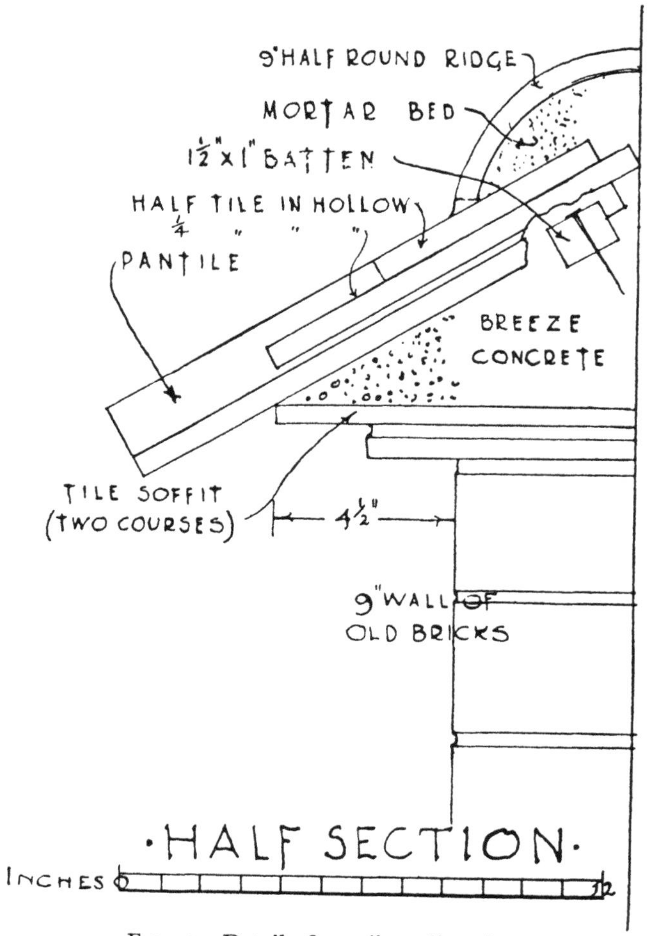

9"HALF ROUND RIDGE

MORTAR BED

1½"X1" BATTEN

HALF TILE IN HOLLOW
¼ " " "

PANTILE

BREEZE CONCRETE

TILE SOFFIT (TWO COURSES)

4½"

9" WALL OF OLD BRICKS

·HALF SECTION·

INCHES

FIG. 27. Detail of pantile wall coping.

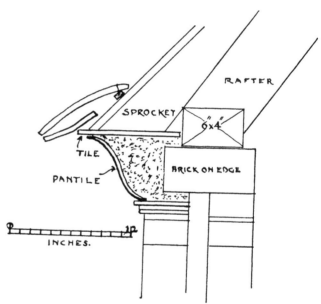

RAFTER

SPROCKET

6"x4"

TILE

BRICK ON EDGE

PANTILE

INCHES.

FIG. 28. Pantile fascia.

II. WEATHER-TILING

Weather-tiling or wall-tiling is a device largely employed in the South of England, where it has long been used to protect the walls of old timber and plaster buildings from wet. It is also used for modern work, and, where building bye-laws permit, tiles are hung on battens nailed to timber framing;

swept to a bellcast by a projecting brick king-closer course also on edge. It should be observed that immediately above this is a course of 2 in. or thinner bricks, laid flat, that the joint may come at a convenient height for nailing the upper eaves course. Both eaves course tiles should be bedded in

FIG. 29. Sheet lead apron in process of covering with heading course of short tiles.

the inside of the framing being lathed and plastered. When the studs of the framing are covered with a continuous and overlapping layer of roofing felt before the battens are nailed to them, the air cavities enclosed make the walls excellent non-conductors of heat and cold.

Another method is to build walls of brick on edge in Flemish bond (as shown at first-floor level in the drawing fig. 31), and to nail the tiles to the mortar joints, which gives the tiling a gauge of 4½ in. The brickwork may be in ordinary lime mortar or in cement and cinders, forming breeze joints, which take and hold nails well, but lime mortar gauged with between one and two gallons of cement to a yard of mortar (composed of one part grey lime to three parts sharp sand) is stronger and will hold the tile nails securely. This drawing shows the eaves of the weather-tiling

FIG. 30. Alternate courses of plain and fancy tiles.

cement or mortar for greater strength, as the under course (being of short tiles) can only be notched at the sides of the tiles for nailing. The drawing shows a projection of 6½ in. from the drip of the eaves course to the wall face, and this will be found satisfactory at first-floor level. The effect of this projection may be seen in fig. 98. Fig. 32 shows weather-tiling carried down to within 3 ft. of the ground. Here the projection of the eaves has been reduced (very properly) to 2 in. In this illustration the verge (or barge, as old workmen call it) is clearly shown with its undercloak, and attention may be drawn to the way a curved tile has been chosen exactly to the sweep of the bellcast.

Although not essential, it is as well to arrange that the verge faces the less exposed aspect. Care should be taken that the edges of all tiles in the verge are kept free from mortar and are left clean and red. Several of those in the verge illustrated have not had this care. Alternation of red tile-edges and white mortar joints is more pleasing than a verge smeared with mortar, and the point is worth including in the specification. The small pieces of cut tiles, where the eaves course is stopped by the curved undercloak, are quite secure if properly bedded in cement, or the last two tiles of two courses may be cut to wedge shapes, as in fig. 37, or alternatively, tile-and-a-half tiles may be cut to include the small piece. There is danger, however, that a large piece of tile-and-a-half may be too conspicuous.

Where a window is set back from the face of weather-tiling, so that verges show on each side as reveals and there is only 5 in. or less of tiling over the window, this course (over the window and under the roof eaves) must be bedded in cement and the tiles wedged tightly side by side. If supported until the cement has set by a piece of board (as may be seen over the window frame in fig. 12) these tiles will be as secure as any on the wall.

Fig. 33 is an example of bad weather-tiling. The tiles have been bedded in mortar, which shows thin white joints, comparing unfavourably with the shadows in the open

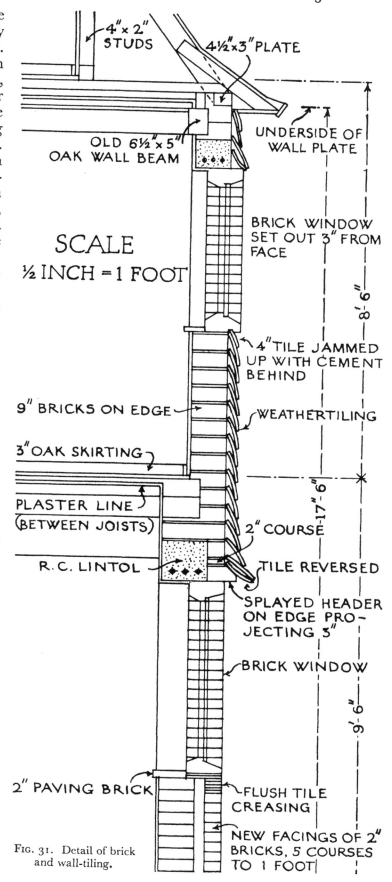

Fig. 31. Detail of brick and wall-tiling.

FIG. 33. Wrong—angle tiles at verge. Excessive projection of eaves.

FIG. 32. Right—treatment of wall-tiling verge and eaves having slight projection.

joints in fig. 32. The tiles themselves lack texture, and the use of mechanical-looking

FIG. 34. Biddenden, Kent. Fancy wall tiles.
Lead apron scalloped.

angle tiles emphasises the sleek, hard effect. The outward sweep or bellcast of the eaves is so excessive as to present a gross appearance.

Fig. 29 shows how lead aprons may be concealed, without their efficiency being affected. The lead is turned up into a throat which is ploughed under the cill sufficiently wide to take it and one tile (see fig. 52). It lies on the last full-length tile course, is deeply vandyked and scored to afford a key for the cement on which the heading tile course is to be bedded. A lump of cement (gauged 3–1, as all cement mortar for tile work) is shown in position, ready for the next tile to be applied. This should butt closely against that just fixed. The result is a neat and thoroughly strong piece of work; the lead being entirely concealed.

There are many forms of fancy tiles, of which two are shown in figs. 30 and 34,

where, undoubtedly, they look charming, but they owe much of that charm to the variety of their own colourings and to the lichens with which they are encrusted. It takes much longer for tiling to mature and acquire vegetable growths on walls than on a roof slope, consequently such fancy tiling will look raw and even fussy for many years longer than would plain tiling. In fig. 34 is an interesting treatment of a lead apron, which (instead of being hidden as in fig. 29) has been scalloped like the tiles and painted white like the window over it, so as to become part of the window design.

Fig. 35 is an eighteenth-century treatment of plain tiles with pieces of white painted

FIG. 35. Tenterden, Kent. Weather- or wall-tiling
and painted wood quoins.

WEATHER-TILING

FIG. 37. Southgate Street, Winchester. The old and right way of cutting end tiles of each course of wall-tiling in gable.

FIG. 36. Angle of wall-tiling; verge treatment at alternate courses. Compare with fig. 32, where verge is on one elevation only.

and chamfered wood board representing quoins, and a moulded and painted bressumer board below. It will be noticed that the frames of the sash windows stop the verges of the weather-tiling.

A departure in treatment of weather-tiling at the external angle of walls is shown in fig. 36, and from another point of view, in fig. 59, where also the tile edges are exposed in alternate courses on each elevation. Fig. 37 shows a treatment applicable to gables, where the two end tiles at the extremities of each course are cut to fan shapes. By this device the use of very small pieces of tile is avoided and a pleasing upward sweep at the roof verges is produced.

III. LEADWORK TO CHIMNEYS

THE treatment of leadwork at the junction of tiled roofs with chimneys or other brickwork is another detail where common practice requires amendment. Such flashings and aprons as those in fig. 38 are frequently seen, though why lead should be laid

FIG. 38. Wrong—Lead eyesores. The oversailing drip course is too high above the roof to be effectual. It should be varied to suit each elevation. See fig. 54.

over tiling (except it be from timidity) it is difficult to conceive. A less objectionable method, which one sees everywhere and which is found in the textbooks, is shown in fig. 43, where the lead of the stepped flashing is exposed on the brickwork but lies under the tiles.

Comparison may be made between the chimneys in figs. 38 and 43, and that in fig. 46, where all lead at the junction of roof and chimney is concealed. Figs. 39, 40, 41, 42 show the method, which is to use at each course a lead soaker, turned up into a joint of the brickwork, like flashings, and it will be convenient to call these "soaker-flashings". The illustrations show two courses and the completed roof may be described as follows: Fig. 39 shows a piece of sheet lead turned at

least $1\frac{1}{2}$ in. into the brick joint, where it has been secured with *two* lead wedges as that shown in the next course, fig. 40, before pointing. The outer edge of the lead is welted to prevent water running over sideways. The cavity under the stepped drip has already been protected by another piece of lead. See illustration of return elevation fig. 44. The sheet lead should lie 4 in. on the tile course below. I may mention that the photographs were taken from scaffolding to a cottage chimney and that the lead used was all old scraps and the job very roughly done.

Fig. 40 shows the next course, where the piece of lead shown in fig. 39 has been covered with a tile notched to pass the brick offset and with a half tile. Here, partly inserted into the joint, one lead wedge may be seen. The piece of lead has not yet been dressed up to the brickwork, and, indeed, is too small, for it does not lie sufficiently far on the tile course below. Its outer edge is also welted—fig. 41 shows this piece of lead covered by a tile and a long half tile, after pointing.

Fig. 42 shows the completed work. Cement mortar has been used to bed tiles on the lead and care has been taken that they shall lie closely against one another.

It will be noticed that small portions of the stepped lead are visible because the man who did the work was not a plumber, but a bricklayer, who turned his lead into joints one course too high and who was handicapped by the thick bricks, which exaggerated this error. The chimney in fig. 46 had all the leadwork done subsequently by a plumber who was accustomed to stepped flashings. He entirely hid his lead and would have done so even had not this been made easy through the bricks being only $2\frac{1}{4}$ in. thick.

The treatment of lead aprons is similar. It is well to build the projecting brick drip course two courses lower than that shown in figs. 44 and 45 (which was an old chimney),

FIG. 40.

FIG. 39.

Lead flashings. Safe and invisible.

FIG. 41.　　　　Lead flashings.　Safe and invisible.　　　　FIG. 42.

so that the heading course of tiling finishes immediately under it as seen in fig. 98. Fig. 44 shows lead at the angle of the chimney before it is dressed in, and also the apron scored

FIG. 43. Lead flashing. The usual disfiguring way.

ready to be covered with two courses of tiles, these tiles being bedded in cement mortar. Fig. 45 shows the completed tile courses, and, as the photograph was taken looking to the left instead of to the right, as fig. 40 (there *are* difficulties in photographing on a high and circumscribed scaffold) the tiles are marked *A*, *B*, *C*, for easy identification.

Probably the photographs and descriptions demonstrate the efficiency of the methods, but it may be of interest to add that they have all stood the test of very exposed situations for many years without allowing a drop of water to pass through. The cost of these soaker-flashings is practically the same as for ordinary stepped flashings. The work may be done by bricklayer, tiler or plumber. I have found the plumber most satisfactory. A plumber who had not done these soaker-flashings before found the leadwork took no longer than stepped flashings would have done, but extra time was expended in cutting tiles to pass offsets of the brickwork. Objection may be made that the concealment of lead opens the door to scamping work, but such objection

would lie equally well against other hidden work, commencing with foundations.

There is one more treatment of roof junctions with brickwork to which I would refer. In old buildings of a humble kind lead was little used on roofs, and the customary cement or mortar pointing (or listing, as it is more correctly termed) at the junction of tiles and brickwork, fig. 47, is an inadequate substitute. It cracks under hot sun and becomes detached from brick or tile. Even when the workman introduces rude decoration upon its surface, with his towel, it is unsightly. A better method (employed in Sussex and probably elsewhere) is known as tile-listing. The tiles are bedded in cement mortar, which is not allowed to show at the joints, and are butted closely together. If the heading course finishes close up to a projecting drip course, neither wet nor frost will penetrate. If the raking courses of the tile-listing are protected by a stepped drip course (all header bricks as the chimney, fig. 53), the appearance is good and the listing

FIG. 44. Secret flashing at angle and secret lead apron.

will be better protected than that on the old chimney, fig. 48, but this listing was bedded ten years ago, and has not required attention since.

Fig. 45. Lead apron—invisible—completed.

Fig. 46. Lead soaker-flashings and apron—invisible.

Fig. 47. Mortar fillet instead of lead—a leaky and perishable method.

Fig. 48. Tile-listing instead of lead—weather-tight and durable.

IV. DORMERS

Of all architectural features, there is none of greater value or which produces such effect of breadth, repose and dignity as a

upper corner of the photograph, sufficient of a two-light dormer is included to show how closely it sits upon the main roof.

FIG. 49. Biddenden, Kent. Eighteenth-century dormers.

great expanse of roof, unbroken by windows of any description. It never fails to appeal to the emotions of the observer, whether he looks at it with the eye of cultivated architectural taste or whether with that of the casual and uninstructed man in the street. Such roofs enclose large spaces, however, and usually they must be made available for bedrooms. For these, dormer windows, if they "sit down" closely on the roof slopes and are well designed and proportioned, are most effective, but (if one may judge from executed work) they present peculiar and difficult problems to designers.

Pedimented dormers of the eighteenth-century type, which are covered with lead, do not come within the scope of this article, but fig. 49 shows two tiled dormers of eighteenth-century date, both of which are good. Fig. 51 is one of Sir Edwin Lutyens' admirable dormers, the design of which must be based upon the stone-slate-covered dormers of the Cotswolds, fig. 156, of which it is an able development. The illustration, fig. 51, shows the upper portion of a four-light dormer, which breaks through the eaves, but in the

FIG. 50. Wrong—Lead eyesores. Cill too high above main roof, open eaves, no bellcast to roof, tiling of cheeks and return mitres raw and clumsy, mortar too obvious.

L B C

FIG. 51. Dormer windows by Sir E. L. Lutyens. Instead of the lowest hip tile being filled with a curved piece, the under eaves course, like the tile soffit, is mitred at the angles and the mitres are covered by tile tongues. See plan, fig. 52. The distance from drip of eaves to oak frame is 8 ins. both at sides and front, as in drawing, fig. 52. Compare with fig. 59, where the projection in front is only 5 in.

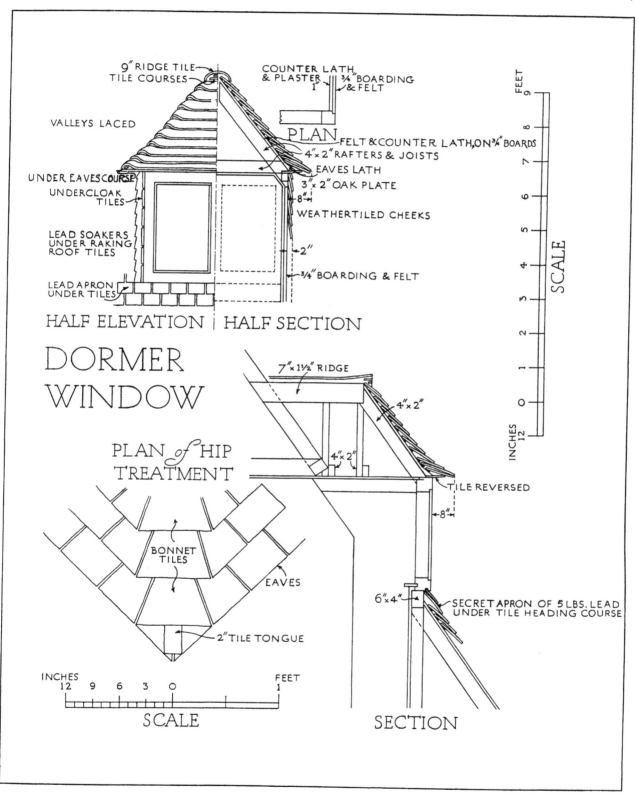

9" RIDGE TILE
TILE COURSES

COUNTER LATH
& PLASTER 1" ¾" BOARDING
& FELT

PLAN

FELT & COUNTER LATH, ON ¾" BOARDS

4" x 2" RAFTERS & JOISTS

EAVES LATH

3" x 2" OAK PLATE

8"

WEATHERTILED CHEEKS

VALLEYS LACED

UNDER EAVES COURSE

UNDERCLOAK
TILES

LEAD SOAKERS
UNDER RAKING
ROOF TILES

2"

¾" BOARDING & FELT

LEAD APRON
UNDER TILES

HALF ELEVATION | HALF SECTION

DORMER
WINDOW

7" x 1½" RIDGE

4" x 2"

4" x 2"

TILE REVERSED

8"

PLAN of HIP
TREATMENT

6" x 4"

SECRET APRON OF 5 LBS. LEAD
UNDER TILE HEADING COURSE

BONNET
TILES

EAVES

2" TILE TONGUE

INCHES
12 9 6 3 0   FEET
                      1

SCALE

SECTION

FEET
9
8
7
6
5 SCALE
4
3
2
1
0
INCHES
12

FIG. 52.

Attention may be drawn to the swept valley; the sweep of ridge up to the main roof and the way in which the last ridge tile is

FIG. 53. Stepped drip courses of chimney up to which roof tiles will come. Oak frame of dormer window showing projection of cill.

carried over the uppermost course of the valley; the gauging of the tiling, so that the hips meet nicely under the ridge; the slight projection of the end ridge tile beyond its plaster filling; the tile tongues at the extremities of the hips; the tile soffit, and under eaves course mitred at the angles; the tiled dormer cheeks, with tile undercloak, behind which are the lead soakers, lying under the main-roof tiling, and to the section of the main-roof eaves, revealed where the dormer cuts through them.

Drawings showing the construction of such dormers are given in fig. 52. The lead apron is turned up into a throat under the cill and lies on the tiles under the heading course, being treated similarly to the lead apron in fig. 29. The dormer shown in fig. 50 is less happy. It betrays the inexperienced hand of

the country workman. It is perched too high above the roof; the filling in of the end of the ridge is clumsy; the ridge lacks upward tilt, either at the front or at its junction with the main roof; the hips also lack bellcast; the open joist ends look unfinished; the return of the cheek tilings on the front is a doubtful expedient and has been made ugly by the coarse, white joints, while the exposure of lead on the main roof is unsightly.

The dormer details given are based upon ordinary practice but these do not exhaust the possibilities of building construction. Before illustrating other methods it may be well to interpolate some remarks respecting detail drawings which may be regarded by the foreman or workman using them, either as guides to show the desired results and the ways by which they are to be obtained,

FIG. 54. Dormer window rough boarded, soffit tiles tailed-in and lead apron set up in throat. The farther dormer before boarding its roof.

FIG. 55. Dormer boarded and felted, tile cheeks completed, tile soffit of eaves in position and composition nails driven in before formation of cement breeze valleys and sprockets.

subject to contingencies, or as blinkers between which he may trot into any quagmire
that may lie in his path, and then as shields
behind which he may take shelter to escape
the consequences of his own negligence, lack
of foresight, and failure to remember that the
drawings may have been made long before the

has to take such tiles as one can get. Plain
tiles vary in thickness from $\frac{3}{8}$ in. to $\frac{5}{8}$ in.—
a difference of $\frac{3}{4}$ in. in the thickness of three
courses—and if the tiles are curved, even
greater thickness will result. If, therefore,
a drawing were made upon the assumption
that $\frac{3}{8}$ in. tiles would be used, and $\frac{5}{8}$ in. tiles

FIG. 56. Dormer window with cement breeze sprockets and valleys instead of wood.

actual materials were selected. The drawing
(fig. 52) of a dormer window furnishes an
instance. In this, the section shows the cill projecting $2\frac{1}{2}$ in. in front of the 6 by 4 in. trimmer,
and the method of finishing the heading
course of the main-roof tiling under the cill is
indicated. It should be remembered that details drawn on the assumption that certain tiles
will be used may prove misleading if thinner or
thicker tiles are afterwards selected—often one

were the only kind procurable, it would be
found impossible properly to house the
heading courses under the cill and (supposing
this was not discovered until other work on
the dormers was far advanced) an incom-
petent foreman might plead, "I followed the
drawing exactly, sir!" Of course, such an
excuse should not be entertained, for it is the
foreman's duty to see that the materials he
has to use tally with the materials contem-

plated in the drawings, and if they do not, to ask for instructions. Usually, I suppose, when work is well advanced and such a position arises, the architect exercises his own ingenuity to extricate the foreman from the dilemma in which he has involved himself. The proper course for the foreman to have pursued, and which competent men (as the one on the job in question) do pursue, is to

well forward as in fig. 53. This illustration includes a chimney, which shows the stepping of drip courses to rake with the roof, the tiles of which will finish close under them. The space to be allowed between these drip courses and the rafters is determined by trial with the actual materials in the same way as was the position of the dormer cills.

Fig. 54 shows two dormers, the farther

FIG. 57. Dormer window showing tiles laid and nailed to breeze sprockets and valleys—valleys laced.

assemble the whole of the roof covering materials on the rafters under the dormer cill to find the exact cill projection required, and cut a wood templet the proper thickness by which to set all the dormer frames.

It happened that the old tiles used on the building illustrated were thick and were curved both in their length and width. Accordingly, the dormer frames were set

before and the nearer after boarding with $\frac{3}{4}$ in. rough boards. The lead for aprons is tucked under the cills: actually, the cills are set on the lead.

Fig. 55 is of a dormer boarded and felted and with weather-tiled cheeks, which include the tile undercloak, and, of course, lead or zinc soakers at rake of main roof. Two courses of galvanised tile nails have been

DORMERS

Fig. 58. Dormer roof, showing lead saddle at intersection of ridge with main roof.

driven into the rough boarding to secure the cement breeze shown in the next figure. The eaves soffit tiles are seen tailed in under the boarding, and also under the hip rafters, which are slightly notched. At the angles, tile-and-a-half tiles have been used, but two

This answers admirably for main-roof valleys but both board and tile-and-a-half tiles are too large neatly to finish valleys between dormers and main roofs, where a 9 in. valley board is wide enough. The tile-and-a-half tiles used measured $10\frac{1}{2}$ by $9\frac{1}{2}$ in. and $13\frac{3}{4}$ in.

FIG. 59. Completed dormer roof: all lead hidden by tiles. The distance from drip of eaves to oak frame is 7 in. at sides but only 5 in. at front. The tiling of cheeks is 2 in. thick so the clear projection all round is 5 in. Compare with fig. 51.

tiles mitred, as shown in the drawing in fig. 52, to my mind, are preferable. The thoroughness of the felting is worthy of note, and in itself, would form an efficient defence against wet.

In figs. 22 and 23 was shown the treatment of valleys laced with tile-and-a-half tiles, laid lozenge fashion on an 11 in. valley board.

from corner to corner. It would have been necessary to cut away three corners to reduce the diagonal to 9 in., but it proved more convenient to dispense altogether with the valley board for these short valleys and to substitute cement breeze (1 part portland cement, 2 parts sand, 3 parts engine smoke-box ashes), which also took the place of the lower courses of tile battens. This material is most adaptable. With it, a pleasing sweep of the bellcast was obtained at the eaves, without recourse to sprocket pieces, eaves laths or tilting fillets, and, of course, the breeze made a strong backing to the soffit tiling. In fig. 56 the breeze in the valley is 9½ in. across—batten to batten—and 11 in. across from the verge of soffit tiles. It is 9 in. across on ridge, and 3¼ in. thick there. This figure also shows the lead apron, vandyked and dressed down ready for the main-roof tile-heading courses. It is better not to tile the roof below the dormer until the dormer tiling is completed, as rain falling on the breeze will stain the tiles on the main roof beneath.

In fig. 57 the tiling of the dormer is half completed. A small piece of sheet lead lies under the lowest course, at its junction with the main roof. Should the tile-and-a-half tiles or any plain tiles be much curved, the corners may easily be pressed into the breeze, which similarly absorbs other inequalities in materials or working.

Fig. 58 is an almost completed dormer roof. At the junction of the ridge with the main roof, a saddle piece of sheet lead, 18 in. square, is laid under the tiles for safety, though not of necessity for the tiling alone is weatherproof: the upper edge of this may be seen in the illustration, which also shows the irregularity of the old tiles. This large illustration should be studied for it shows well-finished details, as the filling in the end of the front ridge tile, the upward tilt of this tile and also of that at the junction with the main roof, the bellcast of hips and all those minutiæ which mark good craftsmanship.

Fig. 59 is the same dormer completed. It will be noticed that the hump in the main roof at the junction of the dormer ridge is very slight; a result which pains were taken to secure.

The art of lacing tile valleys is not generally practised so that at the present time few workmen are acquainted with it, but by practised hands it is done so quickly and surely, and without any cutting of tiles, as to have been employed even for housing schemes (where the necessity for economy is paramount) as the valley illustrated in fig. 22.

V. BRICK CHIMNEY CAPS

Perhaps there is no detail of building construction in which the superiority and adaptability of brick is so marked as in chimneys. Brick chimneys are found in association with

Fig. 60. Early seventeenth-century cap.

timber and plaster and with stone buildings situated in districts where timber or stone are so plentiful as to be practically the only materials used. The convenience of the unit, the ease with which it can be purpose-moulded, axed, rubbed and carved, are factors which have ever caused brick to be favoured, and more than one ancient record exists of workmen being brought from distant counties because they were skilled in the construction of handsome brick chimneys, such as were desired to add as crowning features to some stately house.

Probably the earliest and richest brick chimney extant is that at Thornbury Castle, Gloucestershire, which is dated 1514, but it is impossible to believe that such a highly developed example was the first of its kind. It was followed by many elaborate chimneys during the next 60 years, which are well represented in *A History of English Brickwork*. It is, however, with more simple and homely types that I now propose to deal.

"Sussex" chimneys is a term now used to describe the less elaborate brick chimneys of the sixteenth, seventeenth and eighteenth centuries, which are found also in Surrey, Essex and Kent; perhaps in greater numbers and in more perfect, original condition in the last county, where the hands of the restorer and improver have been less busy. Such chimneys are peculiarly English in their design, material and workmanship, and so charming are these old examples, that it is not surprising they should be imitated in modern buildings. That copies do not always

Fig. 61. Well-proportioned early seventeenth-century chimney.

FIG. 62. A modern adaptation of chimney and cap in fig. 60.

FIG. 63. Reduced projection of the cap (fig. 60) to suit slighter shafts on gables.

prove so satisfactory as their prototypes is not because the latter are unsuited to modern purposes, but because their essential elements have not been appreciated and retained. Besides showing good examples, I therefore propose to illustrate certain bad ones, in the hope that comparison may expose more clearly some of the commoner faults.

In the first place, it should be emphasised that the old builders of these chimneys designed them to be built of bricks of the standard sizes of their times, and, further, that inasmuch as the thicknesses of these bricks varied considerably, they took advantage of this fact and utilised thinner bricks in courses which had the greatest

FIG. 64. Cap by Sir E. L. Lutyens on massive shaft.

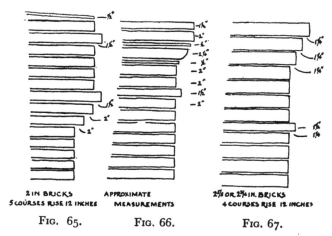

2 IN BRICKS
5 COURSES RISE 12 INCHES

APPROXIMATE
MEASUREMENTS

2⅛ OR 2¼ IN. BRICKS
4 COURSES RISE 12 INCHES

FIG. 65. FIG. 66. FIG. 67.

Fig. 68. Wrong—cap too heavy.

Fig. 69. Right—projection reduced to suit
the same thick bricks as used as in fig. 68.

Fig. 70. Socknersh Manor, Brightling, Sussex.　Good seventeenth-century caps.

projection, or which were isolated: as, for instance, that course which the bricklayer calls the "necking". Those who have read the chapter in *A History of English Brickwork* which treats of brick sizes will recollect that the thickness of bricks from the middle of the sixteenth century until late in the seventeenth

Most of the capitals of chimneys with which we are now concerned are of sixteenth or seventeenth century design. It will be apparent, therefore, that to build caps designed for $2\frac{1}{4}$ in. bricks with bricks $2\frac{3}{4}$ in. thick or even thicker must be disastrous to their proportions. This is the commonest cause of

Fig. 71. Detail of caps in fig. 70.

century was about $2\frac{1}{4}$ in., and that this thickness was established by law in 1571 and again in 1625.

Towards the close of the seventeenth century, the thickness slightly increased, until in 1725 it was fixed by Act of Parliament at $2\frac{1}{2}$ in. for place bricks and $2\frac{5}{8}$ in. for stock bricks, while in 1729 another Act determined the thickness at $2\frac{1}{2}$ in. both for place bricks and stock bricks.

failure, and shows the importance to good architectual practice of intelligent historical study. Another mistake is to put a heavy cap on a thin shaft, and this one continually sees. Unfortunately no one has yet found and published a formula for the proportioning of chimney caps and shafts, and having regard to the diversity of forms, it may be long before such a formula is devised. Meantime, if we would build fine chimneys we must study

FIG. 72. Park Farm, Smarden, Kent. Beautiful chimneys built towards the close of the sixteenth century.

existing examples, record those which are good and note what to avoid in those which are bad. From a great number of measurements and comparisons, the following principles emerge:

(1) The slighter the shaft, the less the projections should be.

(5) A chimney coming through a roof looks best when its longer axis is parallel with that of the ridge (figs. 60, 62, 70), rather than as in figs. 80, 81.

(6) The beauty of a shaft is greatly enhanced by judicious vertical breaks (figs. 60, 70, 73), which are usually of $4\frac{1}{2}$ in., unless

FIG. 73. House at Smarden, Kent. The effect of addition of four crowning courses to the caps in fig. 72.

(2) The thicker the bricks, the less they should project.

(3) A square shaft will take sailing courses having greater projection than a shaft which is wide on one face and narrow on the return.

(4) A chimney shaft on a gable end looks best at right angles to the ridge (figs. 75, 77).

several occur on the same face, when one may be $6\frac{1}{4}$ in. or even 9 in.

(7) Shafts wide on one elevation and very thin on the return will not carry heavy caps. Usually a cap of three sailing courses (and possibly a crowning course) will suffice for these, and the amount of each projection

Fig. 72 A. Detail of caps of chimneys in fig. 72, showing use of plain tiles as fillets.

Fig. 74. Wrong—cap too heavy for gable chimney.

Fig. 75. Right—light cap on gable chimney.

must be carefully considered. Compare figs. 74, 75.

(8) The addition of chimney pots is destructive of design. Where these are used, they should be built within the flues and not allowed to project more than 2 in. above the flaunching, which should have very slight weathering.

In considering the projections of sailing courses, special attention should be given to

Fig. 76. Detail of fig. 74.

Fig. 77. Detail of fig. 75.

Fig. 78. Cap having rounded edges to sailing courses, by Sir E. L. Lutyens.

FIG. 79. Westwell, Tenterden, Kent. Massive chimneys symmetrically disposed.

the effect at the angles. A projection of $1\frac{1}{2}$ in. may look right when viewed in profile, but be found gross and top-heavy when viewed at an angle of 45 deg., for a projection of $1\frac{1}{2}$ in. on face becomes $2\frac{3}{32}$ in. at the angles. Conversely, a projection of 45 deg. at the angles becomes 54 deg. 45 min. on face, and will be found suitable for other capitals besides those of chimneys. The old builders knew this

square of 54 deg. 45 min., which will be found serviceable, also, for testing and drawing caps.

Fig. 60 is a typical Sussex chimney. Having considerable bulk and being built of $2\frac{1}{4}$ in. bricks with $\frac{1}{2}$ in. joints, the cap does not appear top-heavy, although the sailing courses

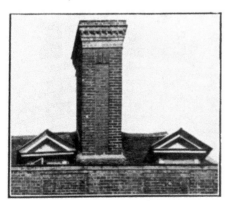

FIG. 80. Detail of fig. 79.

well (though they set out their Doric capitals at 45 deg. in their books), as anyone who has measured up old work of good quality must have learned. In the first chapter mention was made of the convenience of having a set

FIG. 81. Wrong treatment of stack coming through roof.

6-2

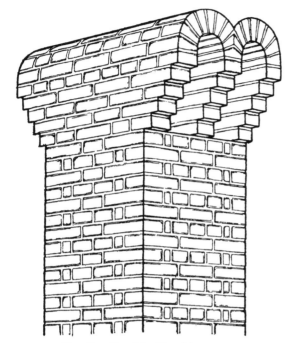

FIG. 82. Hood in Flemish manner.

FIG. 83. Hood with 9 in. quoins.

each project 1½ in. The crowning course, however, is only stepped back 1 in.

Fig. 61 is of a beautifully proportioned external chimney at the same house and built at the same time as fig. 60. The cap is the same, but the shaft being more slender, the sailing courses have only 1 in. projection. Comparison of these two caps shows the attention given by seventeenth-century builders to the variation of projecting courses.

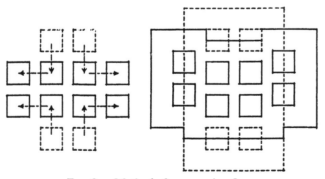

FIG. 84. Method of rearranging flues before coming through roof.

Fig. 63 shows two chimney caps where attempt has been made to copy No. 60. The nearer of the two has sailing courses which project 1¼ in., while in the further cap they

only project 1 in. Having regard to the slightness of the shafts, it was right to reduce the projections, but such deep, heavy caps are quite unsuitable for shafts of this type, as indicated in principle No. 7. They look best from the point of view chosen by

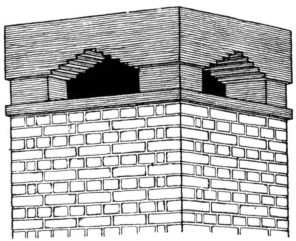

FIG. 85. Hood built of plain tiles.

the photographer; from the front they are clumsy.

Fig. 62 is a modern adaptation of fig. 60, and shows the relation of the fine chimney to the roof and, indeed, to the whole building. The 4½ in. break forward of the front becomes a 4½ in. recess at back, a common device in Sussex (see fig. 84).

Fig. 64 shows the cap of an unusually massive chimney, the shaft of which measures 6 ft. 9 in. by 4 ft. 6 in. The profile, fig. 65, shows how the projections vary, some being as much as 2 in. The bricks are 2 in. thick and joints nearly ½ in.

Fig. 68 is a really bad chimney, having much too heavy a cap, which is built of too thick bricks. The designer seems to have realised his mistakes (which designers do not always do), and in the next house he built the chimney caps have the projections reduced to about ¾ in., as shown in fig. 69.

Figs. 70 and 71 show general and near views (taken with a tele-photo lens) of two chimneys of early seventeenth century date. The bricks are scarcely 2 in. thick, but the projection of the three sailing courses is only 55 deg. *on angle*. The V-rib on the larger chimney will have 6 in. sides.

Fig. 72 shows beautiful chimneys built towards the close of the sixteenth century. The profile (fig. 66) shows that there is one moulded course in the cap. The bricks vary in thickness. The detail photograph, fig. 72 A, shows the use of plain tiles as fillets. Several examples of this fine cap remain at Smarden, Kent.

Fig. 73 shows a house the chimney of which has a similar cap with four extra blocking courses.

Fig. 67 is a profile of a simple cap, which suits square shafts of 2 to 3 ft. sides. Success depends much upon the thickness of the bricks used, and it is important that those for the necking course should not exceed 1½ in. A good effect, however, is obtained even with standard bricks, 2⅝ in. thick, if projections are carefully studied.

The cap (fig. 67) is also a good one for gable chimneys, for which the cap in fig. 76 is altogether too massive. Fig. 74 shows a distant view of this chimney. On the other hand, figs. 75, 77 show distant and near views

of an excellent gable chimney having a well-proportioned cap.

Fig. 79 is a fine brick house and fig. 80 a detail of one of the four great chimneys, varying in bulk but symmetrically disposed, and conferring great distinction upon the whole. The caps have been repointed—possibly reset—but one notices and commends the restraint shown in determining the extent of the sailing-course projections.

Fig. 78 is a chimney where the bricks of the three most prominent courses have been rounded on the edges so that the projections of all sailing courses are as much as 2 in. which would look top-heavy had the bricks been left with square edges. The bricks are 2⅛ in. thick and five courses rise 12½ in. A handsome cap is produced merely by its breaking round the offsets and ribs of the shaft: an admirable instance of ornament—not added—but obtained by constructional means.

Fig. 81 is not a jobbing builder's effort, but was designed in the office of the surveyor to a large corporation. It rises from the middle of a pair of cottages and serves to show how badly such a chimney may be handled. Fig. 84 indicates how the flues of the chimney in fig. 62 were carried up so that the chimney might be axial with the roof.

Where there is a downward lop of wind owing to the positions of trees, higher ground or other buildings, it may be necessary to add hoods to chimneys. These often have been contrived in ingenious forms. Fig. 82 is of a type to be seen on old buildings in Flanders, and will be familiar to those who have visited Bruges. The commonest type in S.E. England is that shown in fig. 83, where the coping bricks are supported by large slates, which bridge the spaces between the piers. It will be obvious that the piers at the quoins must be twice as wide as those intermediate, but one frequently sees hoods of this type where the quoins are lanky. Fig. 85 shows a similar hood built of plain tiles, and is an example of that broad, constructive use of tiles which is always satisfactory.

VI. USES OF BRICK

Arcading, which supports the upper floors of a building, must not only be capable of the load it is to bear but must satisfy the eye by appearing adequate. Cloisters and loggias, known example is the great court of the Certosa di Pavia, near Milan, which has three floors of arcading each receding from that below and each furnished with its

Fig. 86. Prawles, Ewhurst, Sussex. General view of house in which details are embodied.

formed of arches having substantial piers, always prove agreeable architectural treatment. The Italian master-builders of the sixteenth century recognised this, in designing their beautiful and graceful arcades, by varying delicacy of treatment in relation to the weight of the superstructure. The courtyard arcading of the Palazzo Bevilacqua, Bologna, has ground-floor arches twice the span of those of the first floor and proportionately more substantial. A palace in the Via Galliera has ground-floor arcading carrying two upper storeys, but the piercing of the upper floor walls for windows, and the enrichment of these is of a nature which produces an impression of lightness. The great arches of the Ospedale del Ceppo, Pistoia, carry only one upper storey. Another well-

pentice roof. Here the slender shafts of the ground-floor columns look too light, although they do not actually bear the weight of the structure piled up above and beyond them but, actually, only that of their own roof. Even so, it has been necessary to

Fig. 87. Simple brick impost and springing of arches.

provide iron tie rods from the springing of the arches to the inner wall, and from the prevalence of such ties it would appear that architects of this period cut stability very closely in their pursuit of that slenderness and grace which they achieved so successfully in terra-cotta and brick.

and dignified effect is obtained by cloisters treated in this way. Instances of brick arcading with moulded imposts and archivolts in one or other of the Orders are rare —possibly because brick, as a material, itself suggests severer and less sophisticated handling. There are, however, methods inter-

FIG. 88. Section of brick loggia. The capitals and arches of bricks and plain tiles, without any mouldings.

In this country we have a different problem. Our superstructures are heavy, or appear heavy, and, where they are borne on arcading, we look for something solid and adequate. English architects have ever recognised this, and the usual brick treatment consists of gauged arches springing from a simple impost of two or more courses in the manner of fig. 87, indeed it is remarkable what a fine

mediate between the plainest impost of fig. 87 and the full dress of the Order, which are well adapted to brick construction. Indeed, simple, well-proportioned use of brick usually produces better results than elaborate purpose-moulded detail. Such restrained treatment is embodied in the loggia illustrated in figs. 88 to 92, where plain tiles are combined with unmoulded brick in the imposts to suggest more delicate mouldings. The extent of the projections is vital to the success of such design, and these are shown more definitely in the measured drawings, figs. 90 and 91. Attention may be drawn to the considerable effect produced by receding the inner ring of the arch only half-an-inch from the face of the outer ring, which is flush with the

the most important quality they possess (besides their good colour) is their texture, which they owe entirely to the liberal use of coarse sand in moulding.

Although we have so many fine examples of brick mullioned windows, inherited from Tudor and Jacobean times, brick is now infrequently used for such windows in England.

FIG. 89. Loggia arcading. See details figs. 88, 90, 91 and 92.

face of the wall above. The illustration of the inside of the loggia (fig. 92) shows the corresponding treatment within. The offset produced by setting back from 18 in. work to 14 in. work inside has been finished as a cornice with brick on edge, moulded with a bird's-mouth. These bricks are the only moulded bricks used. All the bricks are multi-colour reds, inclining towards plum shades; they are 2 in. thick and five courses rise 12 in. Perhaps

Such modern instances as may be found are usually of ovolo section and often the full, coarse and late section (fig. 93 A) has been chosen. The earlier section (fig. 93 B) is altogether charming, but 93 A, which is tolerable in stone, where joints are far apart, is too coarse-looking when built with mortar joints 2 in. apart. For brick, therefore, the splayed and hollow chamfers (fig. 93 C, D) are more suitable. The windows in figs. 94

LOGGIA *in FACING BRICKS inside and out.*

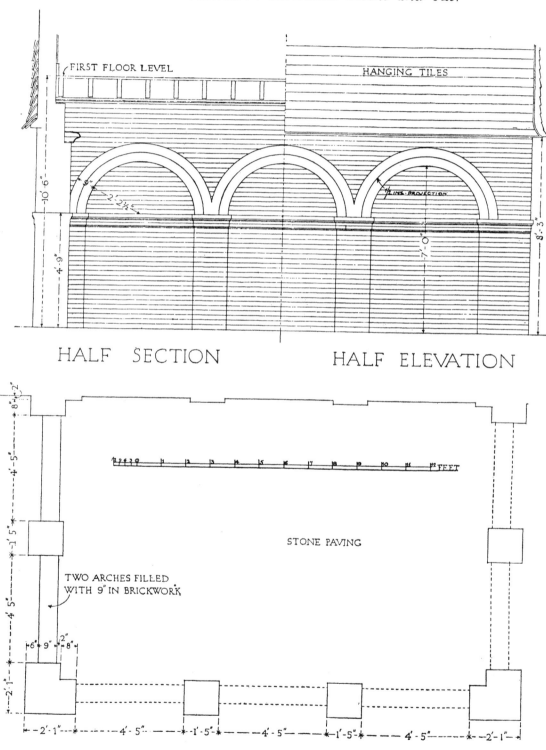

FIRST FLOOR LEVEL

HANGING TILES

10'-6"

9"

2'-2½"

½ INS. PROJECTION

4'-9"

7'-0"

8'-3"

HALF SECTION   HALF ELEVATION

8"-2"

4'-5"

1'-5"

4'-5"

STONE PAVING

1 2 3 4 5 6 7 8 9 10 11 12 13 14 15 16 17 18 19 20 21 22 FEET

TWO ARCHES FILLED
WITH 9" IN BRICKWORK

6" 9" 2" 8"

2'-1"

2'-1" — 4'-5" — 1'-5" — 4'-5" — 1'-5" — 4'-5" — 2'-1"

PLAN

FIG. 90.

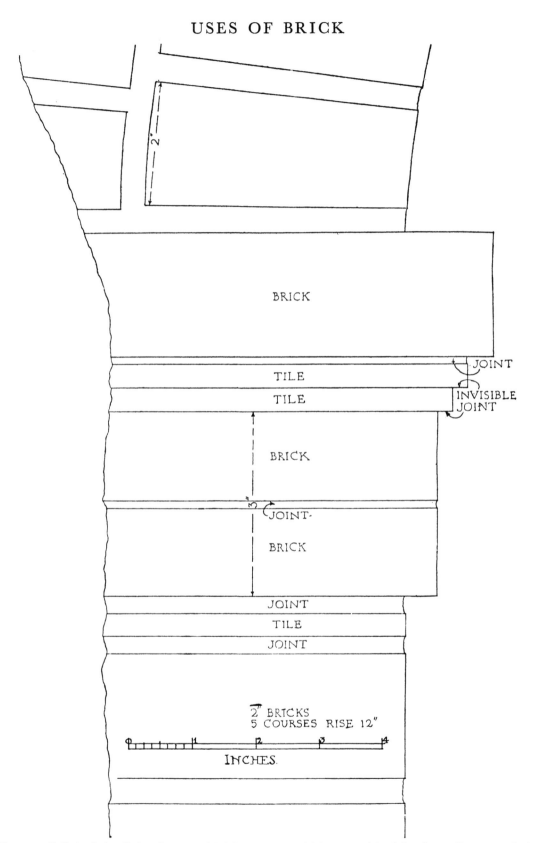

2'

BRICK

TILE
JOINT
TILE
INVISIBLE
JOINT

BRICK

3"

JOINT-

BRICK

JOINT
TILE
JOINT

2" BRICKS
5 COURSES RISE 12"

0 | 1 | 2 | 3 | 4
INCHES.

FIG. 91. Full-sized detail showing use of bricks of several thicknesses with plain tiles to form a capital.

and 95 are of the splayed section. Such bricks can be cut by hand, which are preferable (for hand-cut mouldings have a character and quality of their own), but it is more economical to have them purpose-moulded, as was done for the windows

No. 4 if one angle were filled in. A peculiarity of the window illustrated is that there are mitres only outside, and the splayed chamfers are stopped inside by square-ended headers. The effect produced may be seen in fig. 95; but, perhaps, mitres, as provided outside,

FIG. 92. Brick loggia arcading from within: the cornice of purpose-moulded bird's-mouth bricks.

illustrated. Fig. 97 shows the variety of bricks required. Although there are nine distinct types, the cost of wood moulds (from which sufficient bricks could be made for an ordinary building) is trifling; indeed, some moulds are adaptable for two bricks by a little adjustment—for instance, the mould used for No. 5 brick would serve also for

form a better finish; however, there are the two methods—both sanctioned by tradition. It will be seen (fig. 94) that the mitres are formed on bricks of the same dimensions as the other bricks, and that they are laid upon ordinary headers, showing the horizontal joint between. Sometimes one sees such headers moulded with the mitred bricks.

Had this been done, the combined thickness would have been $4\frac{1}{2}$ in., and, although the result would be a stronger mitre (with consequent fewer breakages before building), the effect is ugly and always to be avoided. Much

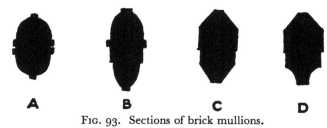

A   B   C   D

FIG. 93. Sections of brick mullions.

of the charm possessed by old brick windows is due to the fact that mitres are built of ordinary bricks, cut as necessary (even into small pieces), and only when one compares these with later large units does one fully realise the importance of the small unit. A purist might even object to the internal-

angle mitres used in the windows illustrated, but as they are cut from the normal-sized brick unit, the criticism loses much of its sting. The bricks used for these windows measure $9\frac{3}{4}$ by $4\frac{5}{8}$ by 2 in., and so are slightly larger than the facing bricks of the walling, which are $9\frac{1}{4}$ by $4\frac{1}{4}$ by 2 in.; consequently, any rectangular bricks required for the windows must be made in a correspondingly large mould, which, however, can be adapted for splayed bricks, as suggested above. Fig. 95 also shows that, inside the windows, bricks laid flat have been used instead of window boards. These should not exceed $1\frac{1}{2}$ in. in thickness (or they will look clumsy), nor project more than $\frac{3}{4}$ in. beyond the finished face of the plaster. Old paving bricks (never square paving tiles) are best for this purpose and look charming if laid with the worn surfaces upwards, which will be found to take beeswax and a high polish

FIG. 94. Brick window—exterior.

FIG. 95. Brick window—interior.

in a short time, when they will present a most attractive surface.

Fig. 98 shows the combination of the roof and window details individually illustrated in the preceding pages. As the weather-tiling is nailed to brick-on-edge walling ($4\frac{1}{2}$ in. gauge), the window dressings could not conveniently be bonded to the walling (fig. 96), but whenever the joints came conveniently, a piece of hoop iron was introduced to tie in.

One seldom sees houses being built with brick cornices. Possibly, that may be well, for they might be ill-done and would be terrible eyesores, yet a good brick cornice is a fine feature, as the able seventeenth and early eighteenth century architects knew well. They built whole "fronts" in one or other of the Orders (the Doric Order was favourite), and these one finds in every brick county. Even where the whole Order was not adopted block cornices were built in gauged brick. One sometimes hears architects, who appreciate rough-textured brickwork,

speak disparagingly of gauged brickwork, and one wonders whether they have really

FIG. 96. $4\frac{1}{2}$ in. wall brickwork for wall-tiling. Window dressings project to stop wall-tiling; cills not yet completed.

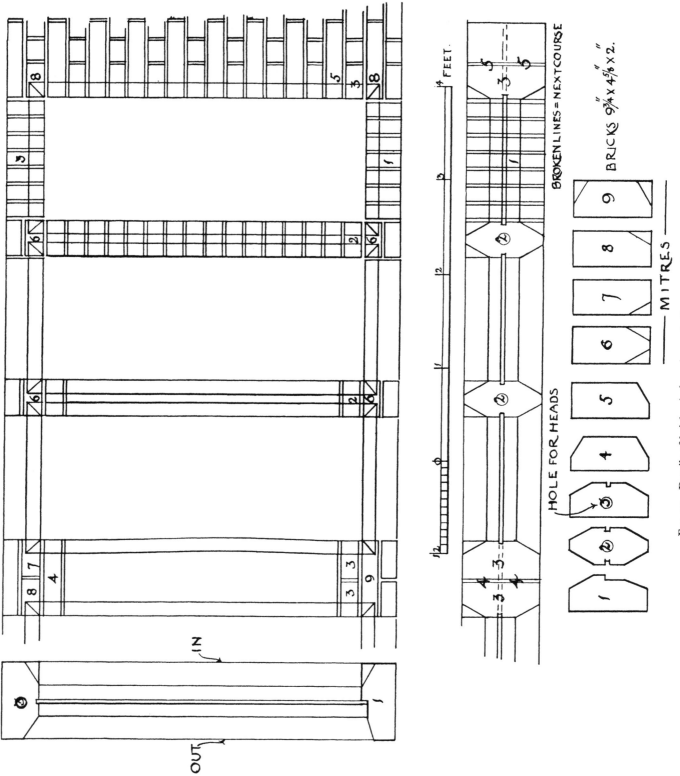

Fig. 97. Details of brick window shown in figs. 94 and 95.

FIG. 98. Portion of elevation showing three types of windows which have been detailed.

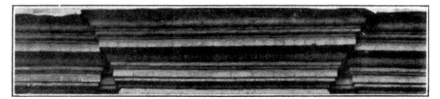

FIG. 99. Cornice at Cromwell House, Highgate Hill, *c.* 1638, showing angle of projection.

studied its use and misuse. There remain with us many admirable examples, and we have still a fair number of bricklayers not only

FIG. 100. **Detail** of cornice at Willmer House, Farnham, *c.* 1718.

capable of building "fronts" in any of the Orders (if furnished with full-size intelligently detailed drawings), but also of cutting all the moulded bricks by hand. There is much hand-cutting in the old cornices, but usually combined with purpose-made bricks. I give two examples, showing what can be done—the main cornice of that remarkable brick

"front", Cromwell House, Highgate Hill (fig. 99), and that of Willmer House, Farnham (fig. 100), perhaps the most beautiful example extant of the Doric Order interpreted in brick.[1] An outstanding element in good brick cornices (some are not very good) is the relation of their projection to their height. As this is exceedingly important and as its importance (if one may judge by certain

[1] Full size detail drawings of these cornices are given in *A History of English Brickwork*.

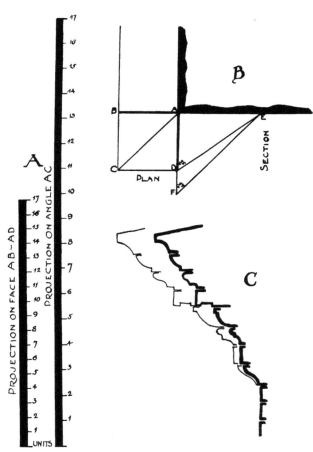

FIG. 101. Diagrams showing effects of projection on face and at angle, to ignore which will produce the clumsy effects often seen.

Fig. 102. Brickwork at Broome Park, Kent.

Fig. 103 a.

Fig. 103 b.

Wall coping by Sir E. L. Lutyens, R.A.

Fɪɢ. 104. **Broome Park, Kent.** Gauged brick ball finial, etc., to brick pier by E. Detmar Blow, F.R.I.B.A.

FIG. 105. School Field Cottages, Sedlescombe, Sussex. Brick steps and ramped retaining walls leading to a pair of brick and tile built cottages. Detail drawing of coping bricks in fig. 106.

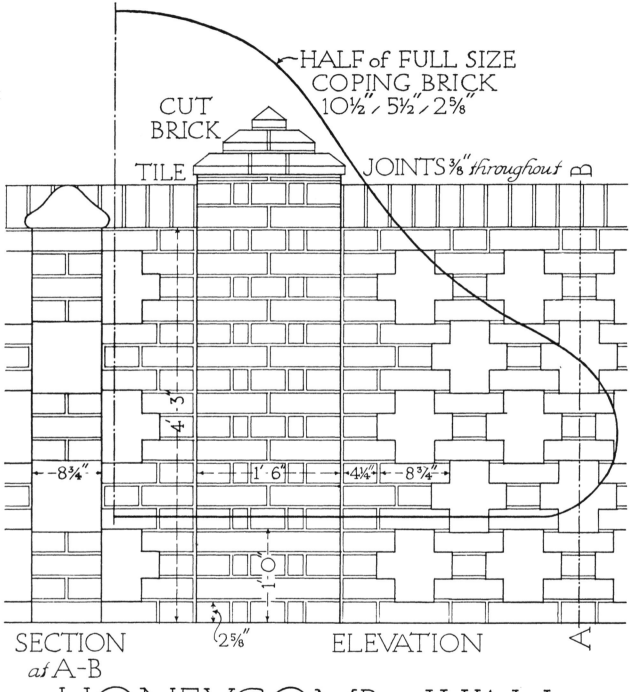

HALF of FULL SIZE
COPING BRICK
10½″, 5½″, 2⅝″

CUT
BRICK

TILE

JOINTS ⅜″ throughout

CUT
BRICK

4′- 3″

8¾″

1′- 6″   4¼″   8¾″

1′- 0″

2⅝″

SECTION
at A-B

ELEVATION

HONEYCOMB WALL

& COPING BRICK   SCALE 1 inch to 1 foot.

Fig. 106.

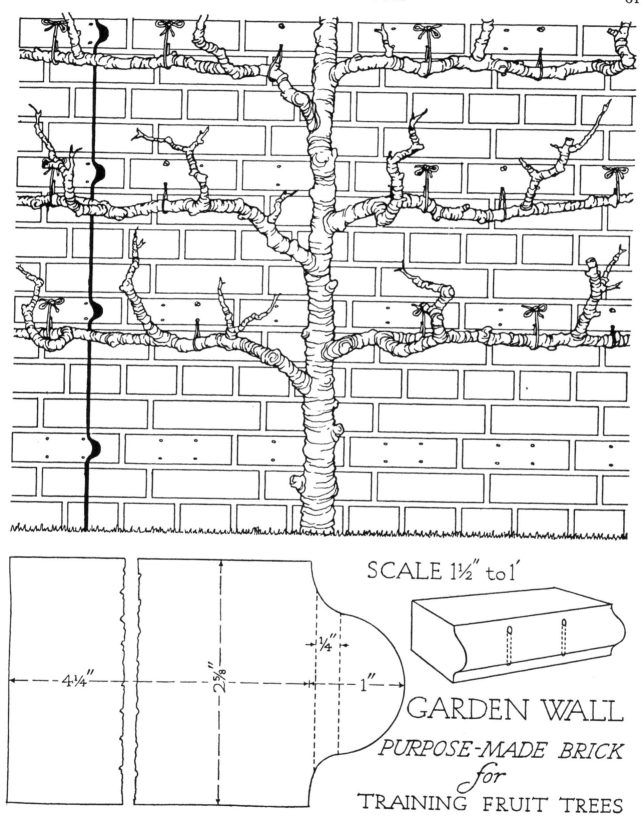

SCALE 1½″ to 1′

GARDEN WALL
PURPOSE-MADE BRICK
for
TRAINING FRUIT TREES

Fig. 107.

modern works) is not everywhere recognised, I venture to develop the point by means of

FIG. 108. Brick-tumbling in seventeenth-century chimney.

the figures in fig. 101, where the columns A show how the projections on face increase on angle, thus: If No. 9 in the shorter column represents the projection of a cornice from the front of a building, then No. 9 in the longer column would represent its projection on angle. This is further shown in the diagram B, where the thickest lines represent the wall. The lines *AB* and *AD* show the projection of the cornice on the two elevations, and the line *AC* its projection across the angle. By turning the page round to read the word "section", we see the same in section. As the lowest member of the cornice begins at *E*, the triangle *ADE* is a section of the cornice on face —mouldings being omitted. The line *AF* is equal in length to the line *AC*, so the triangle *AFE* is a section of the cornice as it appears viewed on angle—viz., from a point at right angles to *AC*. It will be found that a projection from the face of a building, which gives an angle of 55 deg. (actually 54 deg. 44 min. 8 sec.) at *ADE*, gives a cornice with projection of 45 deg. on angle, which is probably the limit permissible. Should the projection on face be as much as to give an angle of 45 deg. at *ADE*, the result would be excessive projection on angle—altogether less pleasing. Strangely enough, almost all the old writers of books on architecture and building draw their cornices at 45 deg. on

FIG. 109. Bricks set on end in concrete to form immovable nosings to steps.

FIG. 110.

face, whereas in the good buildings, in the design of which they must often have participated, the projection on face is about 55 deg. The section C in fig. 101 is from Cromwell House, and is almost exactly 55 deg. on face, which would give 45 deg. on angle. The cornice of Willmer House (fig. 100) has even greater rise to projection, for the angle on face is 60 deg., which gives only about 40 deg. projection on angle. These remarks would apply equally to stone cornices in similar positions,[1] but they have special importance in brick construction, where the relation of rise to projection may also help tailing in.

[1] It is conceivable that it may often be right to exceed these projections for cornices in other positions—e.g. to panelling.

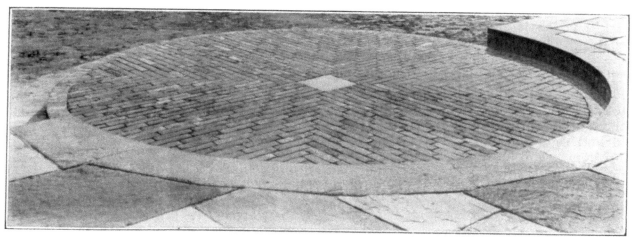

FIG. 111.

Two views of large circular steps built with brick-on-end nosings. The circular step in brick on edge radiating. 12 in. York stone centre.

The possibilities in use of brick for garden architecture seem unlimited. Many examples of old work of this description were included in *A History of English Brickwork*, but more are to be found wherever brick is the local building material. In the new garden at Broome Park, which was designed by Mr Detmar Blow, for the late Lord Kitchener, brick was the principal material used, as befitted the setting of so fine a brick house. Fig. 102 is a general view of this new garden, which will mellow under the master-hand of Time. The detail photograph of one of the brick pier finials (fig. 104) is an astonishing instance of what can be accomplished by a skilled man in cut and moulded brick, which would have appeared to greater advantage had the mortar joints been less glaringly white—sand and lime being more suitable than the putty which is usually associated with finer jointing. The skill with which so perfect a sphere has been fashioned is remarkable, for such balls have proved rocks upon which many a craftsman has foundered. This piece of work is characteristic of the skill possessed by many bricklayers in Kent and Sussex.

Sir Edwin Lutyens delights in the handling of brick. He has mastered the possibilities of the material and fathomed, also, its limitations. One greets with pleasure each new essay from his fertile mind—sometimes recognising an old *motif* in a fresh aspect, often some original adaptation of "common brick", which is altogether- charming. He delights in abundant material. Figs. 103 A, B show the termination of a battered retaining wall, 27 in. thick at ground level and rising to height of 11 ft. The treatment of the splays on each side is interesting. The subject of splays brings brick-tumbling to mind: the old and right treatment of splaying offsets to chimneys and buttresses, fig. 108. It is at once so sound, strong and comely that one wonders why such offsets are ever tiled. Honeycomb walls are frequently seen in various forms in gardens. One variety is shown in fig. 106, together with its purpose-moulded coping brick and pier weathered with cut brick. These are old Sussex details, which for beauty and suitability to purpose are difficult to surpass.

In a Perthshire garden, enclosed by a brick wall (*c.* 1860), apple and pear espaliers are trained. Every fourth course of this wall is built with a purpose-moulded brick, which has a projecting roll, pierced in two places so that a cord may be passed through the holes for tying up the espalier arms. By this means the use of nails and untidy shreds is avoided. The device and its application are shown in fig. 107.

One cannot leave the subject of garden brickwork without reference to steps. Unfortunately, the commonest characteristic of brick steps is that the bricks at the angles and those which serve as nosings become loose in time. I think it was Mr Edwin Gunn who first published[1] the method of building nosings of brick on end, so that the lower ends of the bricks might be bedded securely in the concrete foundation. For steps which are rectangular in plan, I have found it convenient to set six bricks on end at the outside angles, where they form a square panel on the tread, and to fill in the intervening space with stretchers on edge. For circular steps the method is applied as shown in fig. 109, and the same completed in fig. 110, which also shows how some old bricks were used to pave a circular step—viewed also from a better point in fig. 111. In the centre of this step is a 12 in. square of stone. The laying of the bricks on edge, radiating from this, partly straight and partly herringbone fashion, was devised to confine the cutting to those stopped by the bricks on end. These paving bricks were bedded in sand on firm earth, with a view to growing rock plants between the joints.

[1] *Little Things That Matter*, London: Architectural Press.

VII. PLAIN TILES USED WITH BRICK

THE use of plain tiles with brick is of some antiquity. When the tiles vary in thickness, excellent results have been obtained by using them as fillets, with and without visible joints. Figs. 88–91 illustrate the capitals of piers where two thin plain tiles are used as mouldings. The builder of the front of Pocock's School, Rye, fig. 114, axed mouldings on some of his bricks, but all his fillets were worked in tiles. From the street pavement, one does not realise the variety of tile thicknesses employed, some of which are just discernible by close study of the illustration, fig. 114. These fillets are formed of tiles varying from $\frac{3}{8}$ in. to 1 in. in thickness.

FIG. 112. Misuse of tiles. Small pieces of tile in a rough-cast wall.

Modern designers have developed the use of plain tiles for many purposes; indeed, the facility with which this can be done and the adaptability of the unit have frequently produced appalling results. One may safely say that bad architecture in brick or tile is the result, not of imperfections in the materials, but of incompetency of designers. Figs. 112, 113 are particularly unfortunate examples of what have been called "tiddleywinks", a term which aptly describes such fatuous detail, and may serve as a warning how *not* to use tiles. Tiles (ordinary plain tiles) are not well suited for use as quoins because when we specially treat the angles of a building we should do so with a view to producing effects of greater solidity and strength. Consequently, we build rusticated quoins in brick, but if we use a few courses of plain tiles instead of brick, our object is defeated because the slightness of the thin material produces a lighter and weaker effect, which is just the opposite of what we require. Similarly, plain tiles (though often used) are less pleasing than moulded brick

for corbelling out a wall at the base of a gable coping. By contrast with the weak, scattered use of tiles in figs. 112, 113, fig. 116, of a ramp at the end of a garden wall, by Sir Edwin Lutyens, may be studied. There is nothing weak or hesitating here. Another instance of the handling of tiles by the same able hands is given in fig. 118, and in the drawings figs. 119, 120. Here tiles have been employed as inlay or filling of the spandrels, and I should like particularly to point out that this is done in the plainest and most

FIG. 113. Instances of the misuse of tiles.

simple way possible, because one notices that such work is often made complicated by cutting the tiles into small pieces and arranging in patterns, so that instead of that restfulness and breadth at which the designer should aim, the eye is distressed by fussy detail. Another simple and exceedingly effective use of plain tiles is in building piers, as for the loggia, fig. 123. Building alternate stretchers and headers produces a 17 in. pier having a cavity, which may be filled up with concrete if desired, but for most purposes the pier is sufficiently strong without. If all the tiles are not straight but are used just as they come to hand, a certain liveliness and freedom from mechanical monotony will be secured. Curved tiles should also be picked in fig. 122, and have a decorative effect certainly not possessed by the commercial ventilator grid, whether this be of iron or burnt clay. Valley tiles, inverted, can be used on sloping roofs over ventilation shafts from

FIG. 114. Pocock's School, Rye. Tiles, varying from ⅜ in. to 1 in. in thickness used as fillets.

to outline the spandrel-filling on the back of the brick arch shown in figs. 118, 119.

Ventilators of all kinds—to cavity walls, air inlets, V.S.P. vents (where these are carried up in separate brick flues in a chimney, as in fig. 121) may be formed of small pieces of plain tiles built up as shown larders, etc., as those in fig. 115. Plain tiles set on edge, with deep open joints, to be filled up with soil and small plants, make pleasant variety of paving, as used with York stone in figs. 117, 118. Such tiles on edge having mortar joints flush with the surface also form good hearths.

FIG. 115. Valley tiles reversed to cover air shafts.

FIG. 116. Tile ramp and tile coping by
Sir Edwin L. Lutyens, R.A.

FIG. 117. Tiles on edge used with York pavings. Sir Edwin L. Lutyens, R.A.

FIG. 118. Plain tiles as risers to steps and in arch spandrels, by Sir Edwin L. Lutyens, R.A.

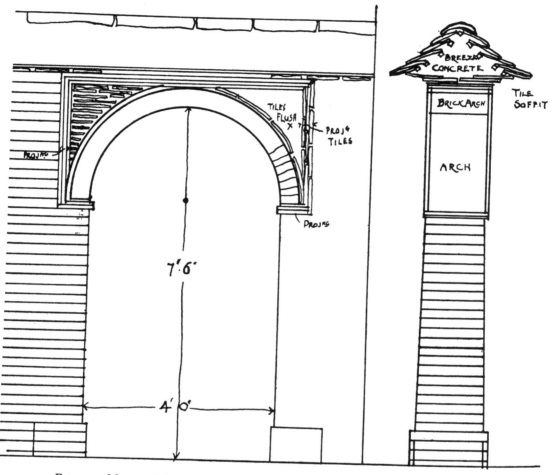

FIG. 119. Measured detail of archway in fig. 118.

FIG. 120. Section.

FIG. 121. Tile ventilator to V.S.P. carried up in special flue. Sir Edwin L. Lutyens, R.A.

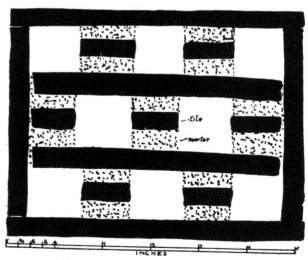

FIG. 122. Detail of a tile ventilator.

Fig. 123.   Piers built of plain tiles, having joints of the same thickness, by Sir Edwin L. Lutyens, R.A.

VIII. BRICK AND TILE FIREPLACES

PERHAPS the most fashionable use of brick and tile at the present time is in the construction of fireplaces, some of which are both fearful and wonderful, probably because such designing is so very easy. The usual cause is buildings of what may be styled the farm-house type, they are in keeping, but in rooms which are decorated with painted woodwork, dainty wall hangings, and such highly developed treatment, they are so out of place

FIG. 124. Norfolk—Oxburgh Hall, built 1482. Brick fireplace in King's Chamber. A typical fifteenth and sixteenth century brick fireplace, of which many exist. (From *A History of English Brickwork*.)

that far too great variety of detail is crowded into a design, consequently in one fireplace so many variations of units and of arrangement are introduced that the eye is dazzled and distressed. Attempts to produce "quaint", "old-fashioned", "old world", and similar effects reek of "Wardour Street", and should be avoided. It must be remembered, also, that brick fireplaces are rough and un-sophisticated in their origin and nature. In as to strike a discordant note. They are best associated with rough plaster walls.

The earliest brick fireplaces are of late fifteenth-century date, but most were built during the sixteenth and early seventeenth centuries. There was little variety of design. They were usually in the form of a four-centred arch, moulded on the chamfer and stopped; these mouldings and stops following contemporary work in stone and wood. A

FIG. 125. A simple form of brick fireplace.

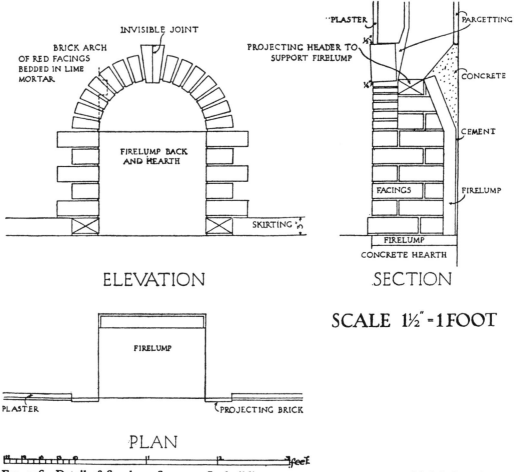

FIG. 126. Detail of fireplace, fig. 125. In building, two more courses were added below the springing of the arch: as shown in the photograph, fig. 125.

FIG. 127. Brick and tiles hob fireplace and clock bracket.

typical instance exists at Oxburgh Hall, Norfolk, fig. 124. The herring-bone brickwork of the back is later work. The characteristic of these old fireplaces is their simplicity. Plain tiles were often used to line the backs, but these were more frequently set in horizontal courses than herring-bone fashion.

at the back. The fireplace shown in fig. 127 is slightly more elaborate. The hobs are formed of ornamental tiles, in which are embedded the iron bars of the front. The drawing, fig. 128, gives measurements. This fireplace and the clock bracket are constructed of 9 by 4½ by 2 in. red facing bricks

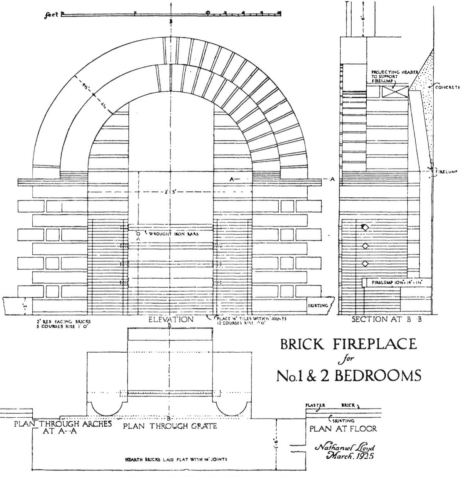

FIG. 128. Detail of fireplace, fig. 127.

In suitable interiors, brick fireplaces are pleasing and decorative features, and are very efficient from the point of view of heat radiation. That illustrated in fig. 125 is preferable to iron stoves usually provided for secondary bedrooms, and, if built with ordinary facing bricks, costs no more. The drawing, fig. 126, furnishes necessary details. Attention may be drawn to the slightly projecting headers which stop the skirting and to those which support the tilted clay lump

of rich colours and good texture. The hobs of the fireplace in fig. 129 are built up of tile-and-a-half tiles finished with floor quarries, on which the moulding has been rubbed by hand. The size of the fuel space was determined by experiment before the hobs were built. At first the fire was tried on the hearth, but the height of the arch was too much above this, and the raised hearth and hobs were built to prevent smoke passing into the room. These proved entirely

Fig. 129. Brick and tile fireplace with oak shelf and brackets. The fire space is restricted but gives out considerable heat.

10-2

satisfactory. These bricks also were 2 in. facings.

The large fireplace shown in fig. 130 is built of small pinkish Dutch bricks (7 in. by 3¼ in. by 1¾ in.) of varying tone and having good texture. The whole of the bricks

seventeenth century date often draw badly, and when the flues are funnel-shaped and the brickwork projects from an external wall, so that it is always cold and often wet, it is very difficult to get an updraught; indeed, such flues seem designed to convey a strong

FIG. 130. Large fireplace of small bricks and plain tiles, where the use of each is definite, direct, and free from niggling or complicated detail.

for the semi-elliptic arch and for the front of shelf were cut by hand. The introduction of tiles for the pilasters provides a little variety. For large hearths such as this, red quarries 8 or 9 in. square are suitable, but for smaller hearths, as that in figs. 125, 127 and 129, bricks laid flat or on edge are more in scale.

Large open fireplaces of sixteenth and

downdraught into the room. In such a case a hood with internal flue was contrived, which extended nearly 5 ft. above the soffit of the oak lintel. This was built of plain tiles, supported by nibs of ornamental tiles, and by iron hoops suspended from three iron holdfasts hung from the chimney breast. Fig. 131 shows the construction, and fig. 132 the completed hood. One foot above the

BRICK AND TILE FIREPLACES

lintel-soffit the work is carried out in bricks instead of in tiles, and 4 ft. above this point the brickwork is splayed outwards on each

tracted flue well up into the old chimney promotes good draught.

Fig. 133 shows a brick hood, supported

FIG. 131. Framework of iron to carry smoke hood and inner flue to be built of plain tiles.

side to seal off the opening on each side of the new internal flue.

Such a hood, being constructional in character, presents a more satisfactory appearance than hoods of sheet iron or sheet brass (such metal hoods always seem thin and flimsy) whilst carrying the new, con-

upon similar iron hoops as that shown in fig. 131, but having only two holdfasts. This hood is built of pinkish Dutch bricks, $6\frac{1}{2}$ by 3 by $1\frac{3}{4}$ in., so is only 3 in. thick. For the first (header) course these little bricks were sufficiently ample, but were too narrow (3 in.) for the second (stretching) course, which

Fig. 132. Completed hood carried on iron framework and fancy tile nibs.

FIG. 133. Brick hood carried on frame similar to that shown in fig. 131.

had to be cut from similar but wider (4 in.) bricks of the same colour. Like the tile hood, fig. 132, this hood was carried up inside the old chimney as an inner flue and splayed out on each side to the walls of the old flue at a height of 8 ft. At a height of 6 ft. from the hearth, at which point the hood flue was sufficiently contracted, a cast iron damper and frame, having opening of 14 by 10 in., was built in, so that the size of the opening could be regulated when a fire was burning and to enable the flue entirely to be closed when there was no fire and a strong current of cold air was passing down the flue into the room. Chimney pots were also built into the old flues, inside the chimney cap, so as to restrict the area of the openings. The effect of these contrivances was to render habitable and comfortable rooms which had been intolerably draughty and smoky.

The instances illustrated do not by any means exhaust the possibilities latent in plain tiles, whether used alone or associated with brick. The examples are merely types of legitimate handling of materials as distinguished from tricky ornamentation having no structural justification and devoid either of utility or of that reticence which is the touchstone of all sound design. Such reticence is conspicuously absent from the majority of those small houses which are springing up in our suburbs and which everywhere desecrate our English countryside. They are seldom designed by architects, but their authors delight in inanities such as those illustrated in figs. 112, 113. It is a relief to pass from such things to contemplate a house built in sober bricks and modestly used plain tiles.

IX. BONDS AND THEIR PRODUCTS

A WITTY Frenchman once observed that although the English had fifty religions they had only one sauce. One might paraphrase this by saying that we have eight thousand architects but only three bonds, and this would be very near the truth, for one seldom sees any other than English, Flemish and stretching bonds. In the United States they

a violation of elementary principles as bricks built on end, while "skintled" brickwork might be the invention of a crazy person who was trying to be original.

Eleven wall bonds, given in *A History of English Brickwork*, are reproduced in fig. 134; ten of which are suitable for everyday work. Where houses are built with 9 in.

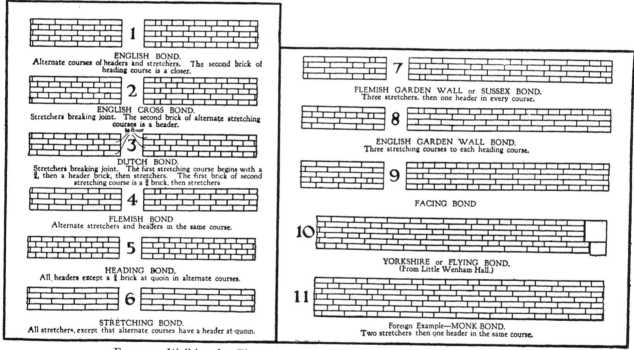

FIG. 134. Wall bonds. Eleven brick bonds, comprising old and new practice.

are more enterprising, and if the enterprise were tempered with discretion it would be commendable. Unfortunately, architects there are not content to exploit every known wall bond, but have used paving patterns in walls, and the effect of herring-bone, basket pattern and similar combinations in wall surfaces is to make one rub one's eyes and wonder how long such obviously weak work will stand. No one who has been brought up to regard bonding as primarily to ensure strong work can fail to be troubled by such

external walls, either English or Flemish bonds (according to the type of building) are generally used, and each is entirely satisfactory. English bond is traditionally associated with brick of rough form and texture, laid with an $\frac{1}{2}$ in. or thicker joint. For Flemish bond a more accurately made brick (having sharp arrises), laid with a $\frac{1}{4}$ in. joint, would be historically correct and, so far as the joints are concerned, would also be right from a practical point of view, because the rougher brick needs a thicker joint to take

FIG. 135. Airlie Gardens, Campden Hill, W. English cross bond or Dutch bond, in which stretcher courses break joint.

FIG. 136. Flemish garden wall bond; also called Sussex bond, with joints so thin as to produce a starved effect.

FIG. 137. At Stanmore, Winchester. Mechanical effect of stretching bond as commonly used for 11 in. walls.

FIG. 138. Flemish garden wall bond built with thick joints (in 11 in. wall) which avoid the mechanical effect of stretching bond.

FIG. 139. At East Meon, Hants. Flemish bond, red stretchers, grey headers, red dressings, gauged and carved work. An interesting early eighteenth-century building.

FIG. 140. Middlefield, Great Shelford, Cambs. Variety of English garden wall bond employed in 11 in. wall by Sir Edwin L. Lutyens, R.A., to avoid the mechanical effect of stretching bond.

FIG. 141. At Chichester, Sussex. Grey headers used amongst red bricks to form panels, etc.

FIG. 142. Modified Monk bond with grey headers, producing vertical bands, some one header wide, some two headers wide.

up the irregularities, whereas the more accurately the brick is made, the thinner the joint that may be employed—an extreme example of this would be gauged work, where the joint is only a fine, sharp line.

There is, however, another bond which may be substituted for English bond, of which, in fact, it is a variation. I refer to Dutch bond or English cross bond, both of which are English bond laid with the stretchers breaking joint: they only differ from one another in the treatment at the quoin, details of which are shown in fig. 134. At some angles, and more or less according to the light, the effect produced is a multitude of little crosses, which are particularly apparent if perpends are strictly kept. This bond has been largely

used for many years in America. In an extensive, unbroken wall surface it is rather distressing, so is better suited to small areas. In this relation it may be observed that there is no reason why one bond only should be used in an elevation. About 1630, English bond and Flemish bonds were used in close proximity—one for ground-floor walling, the other for first-floor, at Raynham Hall, Norfolk. Similarly bonds may be changed in piers and panels, while Dutch bond forms a pleasant variant in gable walls, but care should be taken not to introduce many variations into one elevation.

In cottages, and, indeed, in most small houses, outer brick walls are $4\frac{1}{2}$ in. thick (two $4\frac{1}{2}$ in. skins with 2 in. cavity between forming the 11 in. wall), and where cost is an essential factor (as it usually is) neither English nor Flemish bonds can be used, on account of the cost of cutting and laying so many snap headers; indeed in English bond the number of snap headers to be laid is double the number of stretchers. The usual practice is to build such walls entirely in stretching bond, as in the excellent pair of cottages by

FIG. 143.

FIG. 144.

Two ways of using grey headers in English bond.

Mr Curtis Green, A.R.A., at Stanmore, near Winchester, fig. 137, but this bond is particularly unpleasing, and the more regular the shape and colour of the bricks used, and the more carefully the perpends are kept, the more mechanical it appears. There are two bonds which one would like to see substituted for stretching bond. One of these is bricks, of even colouring, laid with a thin joint. This is about sixty years old and is not a good piece of work; the brick dimensions being too variable for so thin a joint. Fig. 138 shows the same bond used with a better textured brick of more varied colour, built with a full $\frac{1}{2}$ in. joint. Experience shows that contractors reckon little extra for Flemish

FIG. 145. At Blandford, Dorset. Centre panel of grey headers: other walling red bricks in Flemish bond with thin joints.

Flemish garden wall bond, which is often seen in 9 in. garden walls, but seldom elsewhere. It consists of three stretchers to each header—in the same course. In $4\frac{1}{2}$ in. walling, the introduction of a snap header as the fourth brick does not materially increase the cost, but it does just break up the monotony of stretcher bond in large surfaces. Fig. 136 is Flemish garden wall bond in a wall built with sharp arrised garden wall bond over the cost of stretching bond, indeed, it is generally priced at the same rate (possibly because it allows broken bricks to be used up), and certainly it is preferable.

English garden wall bond is seldom used. It, of course, consists of three stretching courses, then a heading course, and so on, as shown in fig. 134. In America they vary this bond by laying five stretching courses to each heading course and call it "common bond". Sir Edwin Lutyens used this bond in a country house some years ago, fig. 140, and the heading courses form softly indicated horizontal bands, which are very agreeable, perhaps because the headers are practically the same colours as the stretchers, so that there is no violent contrast.

A bond which I have never seen used in England, but which has been widely used for centuries in Scandinavia and in Northern

FIG. 146. At Blandford. Centre panel, finely gauged and rubbed red bricks. Dressings, red bricks gauged, but thicker joints. Walling, grey headers.

Germany, is Monk bond. It consists of two stretchers to each header in the same course —No. 11 in fig. 134. It is a bond midway between Flemish bond and Flemish garden wall bond, and is named "Modified Flemish bond" in America, but Monk bond is its name in those countries in which it originated. A wall built in this bond has a zig-zag pattern, which is very obvious in some lights. These chevrons extend several courses high, and as they are formed by association of stretchers, and not by any change of colour, the effect is soft and pleasing. In the 4½ in. outer skin of a cavity wall this bond would not be so

economical as Sussex bond, but it needs only half the number of snap headers that Flemish bond requires. The slightest variation breaks the chevrons, as in fig. 142, where a variety of vertical bands of pale grey headers also has been produced.

The use of grey headers to make patterns is a simple device, long employed by brick builders, but failure to recognise the necessity to avoid strong contrasts has brought this useful variation into disrepute. The old and proper practice was to pick out all bricks that had flared ends and only to use these as headers; the resulting effects were then merely incidental to the bond used. It is well only to use bricks having slightly flared ends, avoiding any so overburnt as to have become deep purple or almost black. Fig. 139 shows such headers, built in Flemish bond. In the illustration they appear lighter than the stretchers because (being slightly vitrified) they reflect light, whereas the red stretchers photograph darker. The contrast in the photograph is therefore much greater than it actually appears when regarding the building. Another use of grey headers is shown in fig. 141, where they divide the wall into panels and (on the left) produce a chequered effect in panels under the windows. Again, the photograph reverses the tones and exaggerates the contrast. In fig. 105 is an effective treatment employed to obtain vertical bands one, two, and three headers wide. In this, as in the brickwork in figs. 139 and 142, the bands are produced without conscious effort by the bricklayer beyond that necessary to use for headers those bricks already picked out for the purpose—he has only to keep his bond. On the other hand, such patterns as those in figs. 143, 144 require constant care and will take correspondingly longer time to execute. A further interesting use of grey headers is shown in fig. 145, where the wall between the pilasters is built with these entirely in heading bond; the walls each side being all red bricks. The centre portion of fig. 146 is of red bricks, gauged and set with very fine joints, producing an even, smooth red surface. On each side of this the window dressings are in red brick having thicker joints; the

FIG. 147. Eighteenth-century house where light headers are used in one storey and dark ones in another, producing variety of effect.

remaining walling is built in grey headers— not very well or carefully done. The contrasts are softer than they appear in the illustration and, with the white painted woodwork and plaster, are pleasing.

Although dark headers are usually best, the rule may be varied by using headers lighter in colour than the stretchers. In fig. 147 one treatment was employed for the ground-floor walling and the other at first floor. The light headers were all red but paler in colour than the stretchers; indeed, some were rubbed to colour. In many Midland counties the normal local brick has light ends, which contrast too strongly with the deeper red stretchers and produce a very ugly and unpleasing effect. There is an old adage to the effect that "a half inch is not much on a day's journey, but is a very great deal on a man's nose". The face of a building is almost as susceptible to slight variations as is the human physiognomy, and failure to appreciate this is the cause of many architectural "crashes". It will be remembered that in the last third of the nineteenth century a bad revival of brick building took the form of making patterns, bands, etc., in bricks of different colours. Thus, a red brick building might have dressings of yellow brick, bands of purple bricks and so on, the results of which were disastrous. Butterfield was responsible for much of this kind of decoration, as in Rugby school buildings.

Everyone is familiar with heading bond used for building walls circular in plan, but it is seldom seen in flat elevations as at the Old Hall, Ormsby St Margaret, Norfolk (fig. 148). Yet its merits were recognised long ago by Batty Langley, who wrote in 1749 "this kind of walling (gauged) when well performed, is of all others the most beautiful, and especially when every course is laid with headers". There must be many modern jobs where such artifices could be revived.

FIG. 148. The Old Hall, Ormsby St Margaret, Norfolk, c. 1735. From *A History of English Brickwork*.

X. STONE SLATE ROOFS

THE use of slabs of stone for roof coverings is almost as old as man himself, and in districts where laminated stone is found near the ground surface, or otherwise accessible, we also find stone slates on the old buildings. No doubt many of the methods applied to tiles (such as swept valleys) originated in stone slate roofing. Unfortunately, local slating in a specification or to direct workmen who have not been brought up in the art. Moreover, slating is a close trade, the secrets of which are kept so carefully as to be a monopoly, and even bricklayers working side by side with slaters know little of their methods.

Stone slates are found and used in many counties—Westmorland, Yorkshire, Sussex,

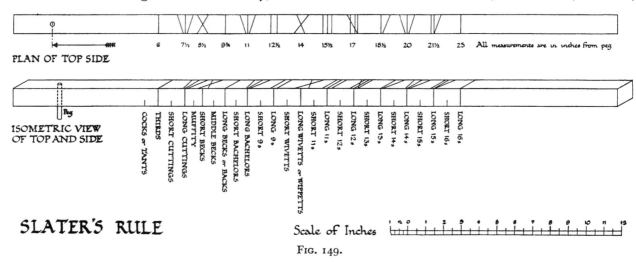

FIG. 149.

materials are now being superseded by natural materials (such as purple slates from Wales) which can be brought from other districts and laid at less expense, or by asbestos tiles or similar coverings which are cheaper and less picturesque. In consequence, the use of stone slates is now confined to better-class work, so that the art of the slater is practised by few workmen, and these generally old men, who are not taking apprentices. Whether this will result in the art being lost in the course of the next generation, or whether the demand for slating in the old manner for better buildings will preserve it, is difficult to foresee, but as there will always be some call for stone slating and as its charm depends upon the way the slates are used, it seems desirable that the stone slater's methods of working should be recorded for the guidance of those who may be called upon to embody stone

and the Cotswold districts each having its own type. The Horsham slates or slabs are exceptionally thick and heavy, as are those in Dorset, as at Corfe Castle, fig. 160, whilst in the Cotswold district roofs are covered, some with large, heavy slates and others with much smaller and thinner ones, just as they may happen to be found in local quarries. Methods vary in each county, as do the slates; but those of the Cotswolds are sufficiently typical of stone slating generally, and perhaps as great a variety of roofs (including hips and valleys) are to be found in this district as in any other. Stonefield quarry slates, as used in the Witney district, are cleft and irregular in shape (often lacking corners), whilst in the Cotswolds slates are larger on the whole and have straight edges which are parallel.

When slates come on a job from the quarry, they are mixed up, and the slater's first task is to sort them into sizes. For this a slater's rule is used. These rules vary slightly (as do the slate sizes) in each locality. The rule is made from a piece of 1 in. by ¾ in. batten, 30 in.

and the significance of these is a trade secret. In the Witney (Oxon) district, from which I have drawn these particulars, there are twenty-six slate sizes, each having its dis-

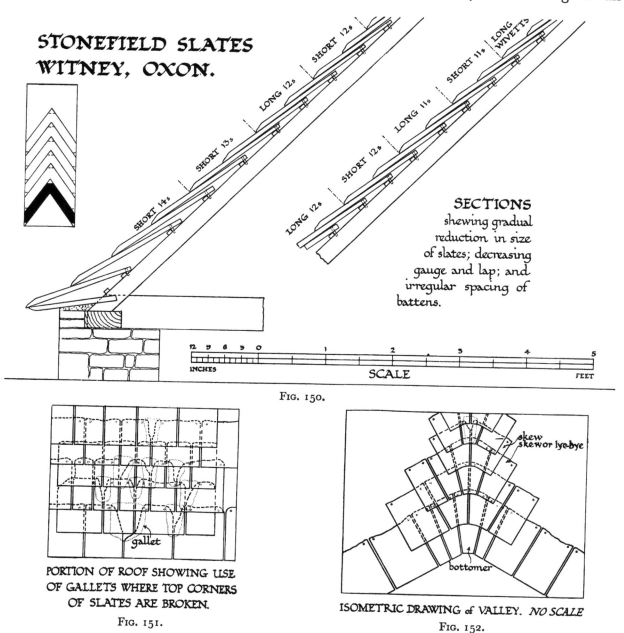

FIG. 150.

FIG. 151.

PORTION OF ROOF SHOWING USE OF GALLETS WHERE TOP CORNERS OF SLATES ARE BROKEN.

ISOMETRIC DRAWING of VALLEY. NO SCALE

FIG. 152.

long planed square. One is shown in plan, and also isometrically, in fig. 149. The peg is put into the hole in the slate and the length of the slate is determined by the notch on the rule to which its tail reaches. There are no numbers or other marks on the rule except the notches,

tinctive name, and each having its length indicated by one of the cabalistic marks on the slater's rule. Beginning with long sixteens[1] (which, by the way, are not 16 in., but

[1] In other districts they have larger slates and begin with long eighteens.

FIG. 153. Cotswold (Burford) large slates, showing two valley courses.

FIG. 154. Swept valley at Witney, Oxon.

FIG. 155. Dormer gable at Little Barrington, Glos., showing swept valley and inverted ridge at junction of gable ridge with main roof.

FIG. 156. Dormer at Burford, Oxon. The slates are mitred at the hips. The end of the ridge is sloped back at the same angle as the roof.

FIG. 157. At Duddington, Northants. A well-swept valley, so regularly are the slates cut and coursed as to imply that such work suggested the laced valleys in tiles, figs. 22, 23 and 57.

23 in. long), these decrease to short elevens (14¾ in. long), and the remaining sizes are known by strange names, as Bachelors, Becks, Muffity or Moveday, Cuttings, Thirds, and, smallest of all, Cocks or Tants.

The names and sizes of Stonefield Quarry slates, measuring from centre of peg hole to tail, in inches, are:

	in.			in.
Long sixteens ...	... 23	Short wivetty or wippetts		13¼
Short sixteens ...	... 22¼	Long nines ...	...	12½
Long fifteens ...	... 21½	Short nines ...	...	11¾
Short fifteens ...	... 20¾	Long bachelors ...	...	11
Long fourteens ...	... 20	Short bachelors ...	...	10½
Short fourteens ...	... 19¼	Long becks or hocks	...	9¾
Long thirteens ...	... 18½	Middle becks ...	...	9¼
Short thirteens ...	... 17¾	Short becks ...	...	8½
Long twelves ...	... 17	Muffity or movedays	...	8
Short twelves ...	... 16¼	Long cuttings ...	...	7½
Long elevens ...	... 15½	Short cuttings ...	...	6¾
Short elevens ...	... 14¾	Thirds	...	6
Long wivetty or wippetts 14		Cocks or tants ...	...	5¼

In the Witney district the pitch of roofs is from 47 deg. to 50 deg., with extremes of 45 deg. and 55 deg. The slight bellcast given at the eaves makes them look steeper than

they are. The verges project about 2½ in., seldom more than 4 in., and the eaves project 5 in. to 6 in. beyond the wall face. Further west one sees roofs having a pitch of 60 deg. In some districts the roof slopes are plain and unbroken between two gable walls. In others one sees hips and valleys and dormer windows, both gabled and hipped. The wall-plate is set well back from the outer face of the wall, fig. 150, sometimes as far back as the inner face. One result of this and of the flatter pitch of the cussome is to produce a slight upward sweep or bellcast at the eaves without the use of sprocket pieces or tilting fillet. This is an important factor in all roofs of old houses in the Cotswolds, Northamptonshire, etc., and is particularly noticeable

FIG. 158. At Great Weldon, Northants. Modern slating with thin slates and lead valley spoil a fine house.

FIG. 159. At Duddington, Northants. A hipped dormer, having the slates mitred at the hips. The ridge is swept up to the main roof steeply, as is the practice in this district.

(as in fig. 161), when the wall plate is set back to the inner face of a thick wall (6 in. further in than shown in fig. 150) and the rafter bird's-mouthed on to it.

The under-eave slate is called a "cussome", which is bedded on the wall in mortar with a pitch of 15 deg., and tails under the first batten, which prevents it tilting (fig. 150). The width of a "cussome" may be anything from 6 in. to 24 in. or more, and thickness 1½ in. Pieces are knocked off the sides to pass the rafters and joists.

The eaves slates are the widest and heaviest of all—18 in. to 24 in. are common, but I have seen one 42 in., and heard of one 60 in. The length is from 10 in. to 36 in.—average about 16 in.—and thickness 1 in. to 1½ in.

The next course after the eaves course is always called the "follower", then come other sizes as sorted out by the slater with the aid of his rule. The laps begin with 3 in. at the foot and reduce to 1 in. at the top of the roof slope. The gauge of the "follower" course is

about 9½ in. Battens are nailed-on three or four courses at a time as work proceeds and as the quantity available of each slate is ascertained. Thus, there may be three courses of 9 in. gauge, two or three courses of 8 in., diminishing to 6 in. halfway up the roof. These would correspond to a "Long Wivetty" or "Short Eleven", of which there might be enough for six or eight courses. Then comes 5 in. gauge, with "Short Nines" or "Long Bachelors". Smaller sizes follow, until at the top of the roof the gauge is no more than 3 in., lap 1 in., and thickness of slates ½ in., with width of 3 in. to 6 in. Frequently a course laid with 7 in. gauge may follow several courses of 5 in. gauge, and this in turn be followed by a couple of courses of 6 in.

Many slates have broken corners which would allow water to pass. To obviate this and still to use such slates, a thin chipping of slate is placed underneath the joint and upon the slate beneath, thus acting as a soaker. This chipping is called a "gallet", fig. 151. The

FIG. 160. At Corfe Castle, Dorset. Hipped dormer covered with large thick stone slates. The valleys swept and all joints pointed. An inverted ridge tile protects the junction of the dormer ridge with the main roof.

selection and placing of these "gallets" require much judgment and experience, especially in the valleys.

The valleys consist of two or three cut
slates in a course, except now and then when
at the bottom of a slope the wider slates require four or five. The centre slate is called
a "bottomer", fig. 152. Those on each side
of the "bottomer" are called "skews", but
in the Cotswolds are known as "lye-byes".
The next course, which breaks joint with the
"bottomer", is worked with two "skews".
Both "bottomer" and "skews" are kept
narrow. Fig. 153 is from a photograph taken
at Burford (Oxon) of a roof in course of
slating. The swept valley in fig. 157 shows
the hand of a skilled slater in the regularity
of its cut slates and their pleasing curves. This
roof should be compared with the modern
roof covering of thin slates shown in fig. 158.

FIG. 161. At Duddington, Northants. Shows slight bellcast
at eaves.

FIG. 162. Chipping Campden, Glos. Pitch of rafters adjusted to bring slating parallel with tabling.

It will be noticed that these valley slates are not hung on pins as are the rectangular slates, but keep their positions by reason of their wedge shapes. None of the slates are bedded, but are pointed or torched with mortar from inside after hanging.

For the poorer class of work (chiefly modern), the ridge or "cresting" is formed with mortar, but the correct "crestings" are sawn from a block of stone, as shown in the plan on fig. 150.

Fig. 154 shows (on the left) stone cresting and (on the right) cresting of cement mortar —doubtless a repair. The valley in this illustration is typical of the irregularity of the work, which, however, is perfectly watertight. Attention may be drawn to the difference in the levels of the eaves. This is a common feature in old work in many counties, see figs. 5 to 8 and reference on p. 4. It is more pleasing in unsymmetrical buildings than when the eaves line is carried at the same level all round. One frequently sees a piece of stone "cresting" inverted and placed at the junction of a dormer or other ridge with a main roof, as in figs. 155, 160. This throws off water to right and left of a vulnerable point.

Hipped dormers are rarer than gabled dormers, but that illustrated in fig. 156 is one of four on a roof at Burford. The hips are mitred, and the end of the ridge is at the same angle as the hipped roof, instead of being vertical. The eaves are very deep. In other respects these dormers might be the prototypes of those finely proportioned ones in plain tiles with which Sir Edwin Lutyens has made us so familiar (fig. 51). In figs. 159, 160 the dormers are covered with larger slates and the ridges are pitched up more steeply to the main roof; this is particularly noticeable in fig. 159 and seems to be the practice in Northamptonshire.

The stone coping of gable walls is termed "tabling". In many instances this is furnished with finials on the kneelers and apices, as in fig. 158. A subtlety in connection with such "tabling" used with the thick stone slates is that the pitch of the rafters must be steeper than that of the gable slope for the tabling. The necessity for this would not arise if the roof covering were pantiles or other units of equal thicknesses, but stone slates starting at the eaves with thickness of $1\frac{1}{4}$ in. to $1\frac{1}{2}$ in. and three slates thick and diminishing to slates $\frac{1}{2}$ in. thick may produce a difference between the thickness of covering at the eaves and that near the ridge of as much as 3 in.; hence the necessity to pitch the rafters more sharply. The slates are swept up to the oversailing tabling so that water may be thrown away from the junction, and this is finished with a cement fillet. This fillet, and the fact that the surface of the slates is parallel with the pitch of the tabling, are shown in fig. 162. Failure in detailing to adjust the respective pitches of rafters and tabling to the slates to be used will produce ugly diverging instead of parallel lines.

INDEX